Advanced Level English

Othello

William Shakespeare

Jealousy, treachery, tragedy and literature's most famous handkerchief...
Othello deals with some pretty serious tissues. We mean issues.

Not to worry. This fantastic CGP Text Guide explains the entire play
— including characters, language, themes, critical responses and more!
It's perfect whether you're an A-Level student or an undergraduate.

We've also included plenty of practice questions, plus brilliant advice on
how to write top-grade essays. Just watch out for that green-eyed monster...

The Text Guide

Contents

Introduction

Section One — Summary and Commentary

Section Two — Characterisation

Section Three — Themes

Section Four — Performance, Structure and Language

Section Five — Context and Critical Responses

Section Six — Writing About 'Othello'

Published by CGP

Editors:
Claire Boulter
Holly Corfield-Carr
Heather Gregson
Anthony Muller
Holly Poynton
Rebecca Tate

Contributors:
Tony Flanagan

With thanks to Luke von Kotze, David Broadbent and John Sanders for the proofreading,
and Laura Jakubowski and Laura Stoney for the copyright research.

Acknowledgements:

_Cover image: Othello and Desdemona in Venice, 1850 (oil on panel) by Chasseriau, Theodore (1819-56)
Louvre, Paris, France/ Giraudon/ The Bridgeman Art Library_

With thanks to iStockphoto.com for permission to use the image on page 1.

With thanks to Getty Images for permission to use the image on page 2.

With thanks to Rex Features for permission to use the images on pages 2, 3, 4, 5 and 26.

With thanks to The Moviestore Collection for permission to use the images on pages 3, 5 and 28.

_With thanks to TopFoto for permission to use the images on pages 3, 6, 8, 11, 13, 15, 16, 19, 21, 23, 24, 30, 32,
34, 42, 46, 48, 52 and 61 © TopFoto_

Page 38 © The Art Archive / Musée Saint Denis Reims / Gianni Dagli Orti

_Page 1: Signature of William Shakespeare (1564-1616) (pen and ink on paper) Private Collection/ Ken Welsh/
The Bridgeman Art Library_

_Page 36: Othello and Desdemona, 1859 (oil on panel) by Maclise, Daniel (1806-70) Private Collection/
Photo © Christie's Images/ The Bridgeman Art Library_

_Page 40: Battle of Lepanto in 1571, illustration from 'Bibliotheque des Croisades' by J-F. Michaud, 1877 (litho)
by Dore, Gustave (1832-83) Private Collection/ Ken Welsh/ The Bridgeman Art Library_

_Page 44: Stage and seating (photo) by Shakespeare's Globe, Southwark, London, UK/ © Peter Phipp/Travelshots/
The Bridgeman Art Library_

Page 59: T.S. Eliot (b/w photo) by English Photographer, (20th century) Private Collection/ The Bridgeman Art Library

Image on page 54 by permission of the Shakespeare Birthplace Trust.

With thanks to Mary Evans Picture Library for permission to use the image on page 57.

ISBN: 978 1 84762 670 7

Printed by Elanders Ltd, Newcastle upon Tyne.
Clipart from Corel®

Based on the classic CGP style created by Richard Parsons.

William Shakespeare and 'Othello'

'Othello' is one of Shakespeare's most Famous Plays

1) *Othello* is a **play** about a respected **black general** in the **Venetian army** who **murders** his **wife** after being convinced that she's **unfaithful**.

2) *Othello* can be seen as a **domestic tragedy** — it focuses on **one man's life** rather than issues of **kingship** or the fate of a **country**.

3) The play's focus has made *Othello* **popular** because the themes of **love**, **jealousy** and **betrayal** are still **relevant** to audiences today.

4) The play is popular with **critics** because it **explores** and **undermines** Elizabethan **stereotypes** about **race** and **gender**.

THE
Tragœdy of Othello,
The Moore of Venice.

As it hath beene diverse times acted at the Globe, *and at the* Black-Friers, *by his Maiesties Seruants.*

Written by VVilliam Shakespeare.

LONDON,
Printed by N. O. for *Thomas Walkley*, and are to be sold at his shop, at the Eagle and Child, in Brittans Burse.
1622.

Shakespeare had a long Dramatic Career

- April 1564 — **Born** in **Stratford-upon-Avon**.
- November 1582 — Aged 18, Shakespeare **marries Anne Hathaway**.
- 1583 — His daughter **Susanna** is born.
- 1585 — Has **twins**, **Hamnet**, a son, and **Judith**, a daughter.
- Early 1590s — Writes his **first plays**, *Richard III* and *Henry VI*, parts 1-3.
- 1594 — His **playing company** 'The **Lord Chamberlain's Men**' is **founded**.
- 1594 / 1595 — *Romeo and Juliet* is first **performed**.
- 1596 — His son **Hamnet dies**.
- 1599 — The **Globe Theatre** is **built**.
- 1600 / 1601 — *Hamlet* is first **performed**.
- 1603 — Writes *Othello*. 'The **Lord Chamberlain's Men**' change their name to 'The **King's Men**' when **James I** takes the **throne**.
- 1604 — *Othello* is first **performed**.
- April 1616 — **Dies** aged 52.

© iStockphoto.com/Claudio Divizia

William Shakespeare
1564 - 1616

Shakespeare was Challenging Traditional Values

Race

Elizabethan literature tended to present other races using **negative stereotypes** — even Shakespeare used **stereotypes** e.g. Aaron in *Titus Andronicus* is a **black man** who's a **villain**. → The character of Othello was the **first portrayal** of a **noble black protagonist** in English literature.

Gender

Women were expected to be **chaste**, **quiet** and **subservient** to their **father** and **husband**. → Desdemona is **outspoken** and **assertive** at the **start** of the play. She was "**half the wooer**" (1.3.174) in her **relationship** with Othello.

Marriage

Marriages were often **arranged** by a woman's **father** — women were expected to **marry** someone of the **same class** and **race**. → Othello and Desdemona's **marriage** went **against** society's **expectations**. Interracial **marriages** were seen as "**unnatural**" (3.3.231).

Historical Background

A *Black Protagonist* would have been *Unusual*

1) In Elizabethan society, **most people** had **stereotyped** views of **other races** — **black people** were seen as **lustful**, **savage** and were associated with **sin**. **Black characters** in Elizabethan literature were usually **villains**.

2) In *Othello*, Shakespeare **challenged stereotypes** by portraying a **black man** as the **noble protagonist** and making Iago, a **white man**, the **villain** of the play.

3) The **plot** of *Othello* was **inspired** by *Un Capitano Moro*, a story by an Italian writer called **Cinthio** (see p.54). The **moral** of Cinthio's story is that it's **unwise** for **European women** to marry men from **other races**, but Shakespeare makes his moral more **ambiguous**.

4) Early audiences would also have been **shocked** to see a **black man** marrying a **white woman**. **Shakespeare** explores the **expectation** that interracial marriages are **unnatural** in his play.

'Othello' is *Set* in both *Venice* and *Cyprus*

1) The **first act** of the play is set in **Venice**, but then the **action** moves to **Cyprus**, which is under threat of **invasion** from the **Turks**.

2) At the **time** Shakespeare was **writing**, Venice was a **great trading power** which was seen as **sophisticated**, **cultured** and **wealthy**.

3) Venice was **widely known** in Europe for its **sexual tolerance**, and Venetian women were often seen as **promiscuous**.

4) Cyprus is an **island** that lived under **Venetian rule**, but was often under **threat** of **invasion** from the **Turks**. It was **isolated**, **war-like** and seen as **uncivilised**. The **problems** between Desdemona and Othello begin **after** they arrive on Cyprus.

© Everett Collection / Rex Features

'Othello' was *Written* for the *Globe Theatre*

This is what the **Globe theatre** might have **looked like**:

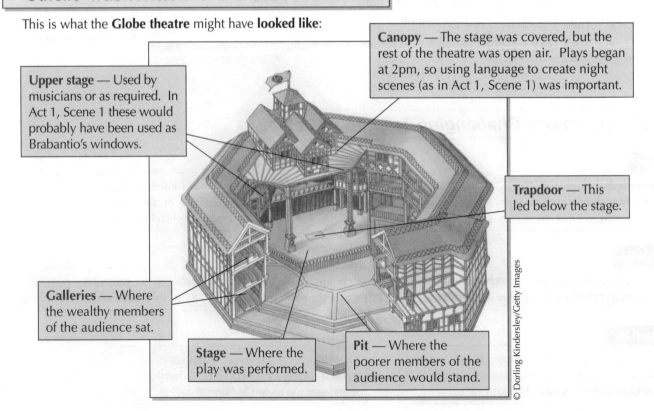

Canopy — The stage was covered, but the rest of the theatre was open air. Plays began at 2pm, so using language to create night scenes (as in Act 1, Scene 1) was important.

Upper stage — Used by musicians or as required. In Act 1, Scene 1 these would probably have been used as Brabantio's windows.

Trapdoor — This led below the stage.

Galleries — Where the wealthy members of the audience sat.

Stage — Where the play was performed.

Pit — Where the poorer members of the audience would stand.

© Dorling Kindersley/Getty Images

Who's Who in 'Othello'

The Cypriots

Montano...
...is the governor of Cyprus before being replaced.

Bianca...
...is a prostitute who lives in Cyprus and is in a relationship with Cassio. She genuinely loves Cassio, but Cassio treats her with contempt.

© Johan Persson / ArenaPAL

Relationship

The Venetian Army

Cassio...
...is Othello's lieutenant, despite being a young and inexperienced soldier. He's handsome, educated and flirtatious. He's also loyal to Othello.

© Johan Persson / ArenaPAL

Married

© Everett Collection / Rex Features

Iago...
...is Othello's ancient (junior army officer) and the play's villain. He's cruel, ruthless and manipulates the other characters.

Othello...
...is a successful general in the Venetian army, and the play's protagonist. He marries Desdemona, but is manipulated by Iago into thinking that she's been unfaithful.

© Moviestore Collection Ltd

Venetian Citizens

The Duke of Venice...
...is the ruler of Venice and is in charge of the army.

© Johan Persson / ArenaPAL

Roderigo...
...is a wealthy but foolish Venetian nobleman who is rejected by Desdemona. He's easily led and materialistic — he thinks he can buy Desdemona's love.

© Colin Willoughby / ArenaPAL

Emilia...
...is Iago's wife and Desdemona's lady-in-waiting. She's cynical about men and relationships. She shows a strong loyalty to both her husband and Desdemona.

Brabantio's Family

Gratiano...
...is Venetian nobility, and Brabantio's brother.

Lodovico...
...is a Venetian nobleman, and Desdemona's cousin.

Brabantio...
...is a Venetian senator, and Desdemona's father. He disowns Desdemona when she marries Othello.

© Johan Persson / ArenaPAL

Desdemona...
...is Brabantio's young and beautiful daughter. She's loyal, loving and obedient, but she shows independence by marrying Othello behind her father's back.

Married

© Alastair Muir / Rex Features

Play Synopsis

'Othello'... what happens when?

Here's a little recap of the <u>main events</u> in *Othello*. There aren't as many deaths as I'd normally like to see, but there are loads of other important little bits, so here's a handy guide so that you'll know roughly where to flick to. No need to thank us...

Act One — Othello has Married Desdemona

> Iago's **plot against Othello** is revealed in Act 1, Scene 3.

- **Iago** talks to **Roderigo** about his **hatred** for **Cassio** and **Othello**. Roderigo has been **paying** Iago to help him **seduce** Desdemona, but she has **secretly married** Othello. Iago persuades Roderigo to tell Desdemona's father, **Brabantio**, about the marriage.

- Brabantio finds Othello and **accuses him** of **stealing** his daughter.

- Brabantio and Othello go to see the **Duke**. The Duke summons **Desdemona**, who says that she **loves** Othello. As a result, Brabantio **disowns** his daughter.

- The Duke **sends Othello** to **defend Cyprus** against the **Turks**. Othello **agrees to** let Desdemona **go with him**, but he asks Iago's wife, **Emilia**, to **look after her**.

- Iago tells Roderigo to come to Cyprus. Alone on stage, Iago then reveals his **plan** to **convince Othello** that Desdemona is **sleeping with** Cassio.

Act Two — Cassio Gets Drunk and Falls Out with Othello

- On the voyage to Cyprus, there is a **huge storm** which destroys the **Turkish fleet**. All of the Venetians **arrive safely**.

- Iago tells Roderigo that Cassio is another **love rival**, and persuades him to **start** a **fight** with **Cassio**.

- After Iago persuades Cassio to **drink**, Cassio gets into a **drunken fight** with Roderigo. During the fight, Cassio **stabs Montano**, the **governor of Cyprus**. Othello **removes Cassio** from his **position**.

- Iago tells Cassio that he should **ask** Desdemona to **speak** to Othello about getting his **job back**.

Act Three — Emilia Steals the Handkerchief

> The **handkerchief plot device** emerges in Act 3, Scene 3.

- Desdemona asks Othello to **reinstate Cassio**. **Iago encourages** Othello to think that Cassio and Desdemona are having an **affair**. At first, Othello **refuses** to **believe** it, but Iago **convinces him** that it's **true**.

- Othello claims that he's **sick**. Desdemona dabs Othello's forehead, but **accidentally drops** her **handkerchief**.

- **Emilia** picks up the handkerchief and gives it to **Iago**. **Alone** on stage, Iago plans to put the handkerchief in Cassio's lodgings.

- Othello asks Iago for **proof** of Desdemona's **infidelity**. Iago tells Othello that he has **seen Cassio** with her **handkerchief**. Othello takes this as **proof** and asks Iago to **murder Cassio** and makes Iago his **lieutenant**.

- Othello **confronts Desdemona** about the handkerchief, but she tries to talk about **Cassio**. Othello **storms off** in **anger**.

- Cassio **asks** his **mistress, Bianca**, to make a **copy** of the **handkerchief**, but Bianca **worries** that Cassio has a **new lover**.

Act Four — Othello Starts to Lose Control of Himself

- Iago continues to **convince Othello** of Desdemona's **affair**.
- Othello's **madness** becomes more **severe** and he falls into a **fit**. Cassio enters and Iago tells him that Othello is **unwell**. Iago tells Cassio to **return shortly**, and Cassio **leaves**.
- Iago persuades Othello to **eavesdrop** on Cassio. When Cassio **returns**, he jokes with Iago about how much **Bianca** loves him, but Othello **thinks** that they are talking about **Desdemona**.
- Bianca enters and **angrily returns** the handkerchief to Cassio. This **convinces Othello** that Desdemona has been **unfaithful**.
- Bianca leaves and Cassio follows. Othello again tells Iago to **kill Cassio**, and reveals that he **plans** to **murder Desdemona**.

- **Lodovico** enters with **news** that Othello is to **return home**, and that **Cassio** is to take Othello's place as **governor of Cyprus**. Othello **strikes Desdemona** in a rage in front of Lodovico.
- Othello **accuses Desdemona** of being **unfaithful**, but Desdemona **denies** doing **anything wrong**.
- Roderigo **confronts Iago** about his **lack of success** with Desdemona. Iago **convinces Roderigo** that **killing Cassio** will help him **seduce** Desdemona.

Act Five — Othello Finds Out the Truth but it's Too Late

Othello's **jealousy** leads him to **kill Desdemona** in Act 5, Scene 2.

- In a **fight** organised by **Iago**, Roderigo tries to **stab** Cassio but **misses**, and Cassio **injures Roderigo** instead. Iago **secretly stabs** Cassio and leaves.
- Lodovico, Gratiano and Iago find Roderigo and Cassio **bleeding**. Iago **pretends** to **help**, but secretly **stabs** and **kills Roderigo** so that he **can't reveal** the **truth**.
- Bianca enters, and Iago **blames her** for the **attack**.
- In a **soliloquy**, Othello resolves to **kill Desdemona** as she **sleeps** in their **marriage bed**. He wakes her and tells her that he's going to **kill her**. Desdemona **denies** being **unfaithful** but Othello **smothers her**.

- Desdemona's **murder** is **discovered** by Emilia, Montano, Gratiano and Iago. When Emilia finds out that Othello killed Desdemona because of the **handkerchief**, she reveals that **Iago is responsible**.
- Iago **kills Emilia**, then **runs away**. Montano and Gratiano **give chase**, and return with Iago, Lodovico and Cassio. Othello **wounds Iago** and **admits** that he **ordered Cassio** to be **killed**.
- Cassio and Lodovico **produce letters** written by Roderigo that **prove Iago's guilt**, but Iago **refuses to talk**.
- Lodovico tells Othello he must go on **trial** for his **crimes**, but Othello **refuses** and **kills himself**. Lodovico announces that **Cassio** will be **made governor**, then **returns to Venice** to tell the **Duke** what has **happened**.

'Othello' — not just another play about jealousy...

Okay, so there *is* a lot of jealousy, but *Othello* is also jammed full of other stuff — famous quotations, unanswered questions, thematic concerns — all thanks to Shakey himself. Oh well... lucky for you, we've got another 64 pages in which to cover all the really important bits. Plus, there's a cartoon at the back of the book...

Act 1, Scene 1

The play opens on the streets of Venice at night — there seems to be tension in the air.

Iago and Roderigo **Discuss Othello**...

- Roderigo has **paid** Iago to help him win **Desdemona's love**. Roderigo's angry because she's **married Othello**.
- Iago tells Roderigo that he **hates Othello** for promoting **Cassio** to lieutenant ahead of him.
- They wake up Desdemona's father, **Brabantio**, and tell him about her **secret marriage** to Othello.
- Brabantio is **furious** when he discovers that she's **run away**. He goes with Roderigo to **confront** Othello.

This scene **sets** a **tone** of **confusion** and **conflict** for the rest of the play:

1) Scene 1 begins **mid-conversation** — the **audience** has **no idea** what Iago and Roderigo are talking about. They discuss **Othello** in **crude** and **critical** terms but they never use his **name**, which **increases** the audience's confusion.

2) The sense of **uncertainty** is **emphasised** as the action takes place at **night** — Iago tells Roderigo to "**Rouse**" Brabantio from his **sleep** (line 69). The **darkness** links to a **metaphorical** difficulty in **seeing** — this becomes a **theme** in the play as the characters **struggle to separate** appearances from reality.

3) There's also lots of **conflict** in this scene — in the opening lines, Iago and Roderigo appear **argumentative**, then Brabantio becomes **angry**. This **tense atmosphere anticipates** the **disputes later** in the play. It also shows from the very **beginning** that Iago is **skilled** in creating **disorder** and **taking advantage** of situations.

Iago is **Deceptive** and **Manipulative**

> An antagonist is a character who provides opposition to the protagonist (in this case Othello).

Shakespeare suggests that Iago will be the play's **antagonist**, even **before** Othello **appears** on stage:

1) He **openly admits** that he's **deceptive** and **selfish**, saying "**In following him, I follow but myself**" (line 59). His **language** is full of **imagery** of **disease** and **poison** — phrases like "**poison his delight**" (line 69) and "**Plague him with flies**" (line 72) suggest he has a **darker purpose**.

2) Iago tells Roderigo "**I am not what I am**" (line 66) — there's an **inconsistency** between how he **appears** and what he's **really like**. This introduces Iago's **mysterious nature** and his **unwillingness** to share his **true thoughts** (see p.26).

3) Iago **helps** Roderigo to wake Brabantio, then **leaves** to maintain the **appearance** of **loyalty** to Othello: "**I must show out a flag and sign of love**" (line 157). This suggests that Iago manipulates people from **behind the scenes** — he's willing to **use other people** to **maintain** his **reputation** of being **honest**.

4) Iago uses **language** to **manipulate** Brabantio — he **identifies** Brabantio's **fears** and **preys** on them. By repeating "**thieves**" four times (lines 80-82) he **encourages** Brabantio to feel that Othello has **stolen** his daughter, and he uses **bestial**, **sexual language** to **exaggerate** the **sinfulness** of the marriage.

© Johan Persson / ArenaPAL

This scene **Introduces** some **Key Themes**

> Lascivious means having an indecent or intense sexual desire.

Jealousy

Iago is **jealous** of Cassio's new position as Othello's **lieutenant**. He **questions** Cassio's **abilities** as a **soldier**, and **challenges** his **masculinity**, by saying that he's got no more knowledge of war than "**a spinster**" (line 24). The **alliteration** of "**prattle without practice**" (line 26) emphasises his contempt.

Sexuality

This scene is full of **sexual language**, e.g. Iago says Othello and Desdemona are "**making the beast with two backs**" (lines 117-118). Iago's references to sex involve **animal imagery** — he makes their **union** seem **crude** and **unnatural**.

Honesty and Deception

Iago says that he's deceiving Othello, but **Othello** and **Desdemona** have also deceived Brabantio by **eloping**. Even the characters who seem **honest** are capable of **dishonesty**.

Racism

The characters use **racist language** to describe Othello. Roderigo calls him "**the thick-lips**" (line 67), and **animalistic imagery** presents Othello as **different** and **uncivilised**. He's called a "**devil**" (line 92) and a "**lascivious Moor**" (line 127), which shows how Othello is **defined** by his **race**, **unlike** the other, **white**, characters.

Act 1, Scene 2

On another Venetian street Iago meets with Othello — the audience sees the target of Iago's hate for the first time...

Brabantio **Accuses** Othello of **Stealing** his daughter...

- Iago **warns** Othello that his **secret marriage** to Desdemona has been **discovered**.
- Othello is **summoned** to see the **Duke** to discuss the situation in **Cyprus**.
- Brabantio enters and **accuses Othello**. Brabantio decides to bring the **case** before the **Duke**.

In line 33, Iago associates himself with "Janus", a two-faced Roman god. This emphasises his two-faced nature.

Scene 2 **builds** on what the audience has learned in **Scene 1** about Iago's **hypocritical nature**:

1) The audience sees that **Iago** can **adapt** to suit any situation. At the beginning of Scene 2 he **reverses** his alliances — he calls Othello "**sir**" and threatens to **attack** Roderigo: "**Come, sir, I am for you**" (line 58).

2) Iago's **hypocrisy** is **shown** when he **criticises Brabantio** for the "**provoking terms**" (line 7) he used to talk about Othello and says he should have "**yerked**" (**stabbed**) Brabantio for it (line 5). This provides **dramatic irony** because Iago **encouraged** Brabantio — it's clear that Iago **causes conflict** and can't be **trusted**.

Othello is **Very Different** from how he's **Described**

There's a **stark contrast** between how Othello is **described**, and how he **acts** in Scene 2:

He's described as...
- proud and selfish —"**loving his own pride and purposes**" (1.1.12).
- sexual — "**lascivious**" (1.1.127).
- a savage, uncivilised "**thing**" (line 71), an "**old black ram**" and a "**devil**" (1.1.89-92).
- immoral — a "**foul thief**" (line 62) using "**foul charms**" (line 73).

But in this scene he is...
- aware (and **proud**) of the **service** he has done for Venice. He **defends himself** against Brabantio's **attacks** on his **reputation**, and **believes** he has a "**perfect soul**" (line 31).
- in love with Desdemona —"**I love the gentle Desdemona**" (line 25). He doesn't mention **lust** or his **sexual desires**.
- **controlled** — he **avoids violence**, defusing the situation by saying "**Keep up your bright swords, for the dew will rust them**" (line 59). His behaviour **contradicts** the **racist slurs**.
- **open** about his **actions** — he says to Brabantio that he's **willing** to "**answer this your charge**" (line 85).

Othello's **language** is **eloquent**, even after Brabantio's insults — he's the **first** character to speak **calmly** in the play.

Brabantio **Presents** Othello and Desdemona's **Love** as **Unnatural**

The marriage of a **black man** and a **white woman** was seen as **unnatural** in Elizabethan England — people were **expected** to marry someone of the **same race** and **class**. Shakespeare **explores** this through Brabantio's **objections**:

1) Brabantio's **main objection** is Othello's **race** — he uses racist language, describing Othello's "**sooty bosom**", and **dehumanising** him by calling him a "**thing**" (lines 70-71) .

2) Brabantio accuses Othello of **binding** Desdemona in "**chains of magic**" (line 65) to force her into marriage. By using the **language** of **witchcraft**, he shows that he **can't imagine** that she would **marry** Othello through her own **choice**. He **thinks** that Desdemona should "**fear**" Othello, rather than "**delight**" in him (line 71).

3) The **rhyming couplet** at the end of the scene emphasises Brabantio's view that Othello's marriage to Desdemona has turned the world **upside-down**: "**Bondslaves**" will become "**statesmen**" (line 99).

Practice Questions

Q1 Compare the impression the audience has of Othello after Scene 1 with the impression they have after Scene 2.

Q2 How does Shakespeare present Iago's character traits in the first two scenes of *Othello*? Refer to the text in your answer.

"Even now, now, very now, an old black ram / Is tupping your white ewe"

When I look at quotes like this I do wonder if Shakespeare occasionally just used filler words to flesh out his iambic pentameters — 'Do you agree? Yes, yea verily yes? / Or disagree, no, nada, not at all?' I'm at least half as good as he ever was...

Act 1, Scene 3

Scene 3 takes place in a council chamber in Venice. The Duke and his senators are discussing a war against the Turks.

Othello *and* Desdemona *explain how they fell in* Love...

- The **Duke** is discussing the **military situation** in **Cyprus** with his senators. They tell Othello to **prepare** for **war**.
- Brabantio **accuses** Othello of **stealing** Desdemona from him. The Duke asks for **evidence**. Othello and Desdemona **explain** how they fell in **love** — this **convinces** the Duke, but Brabantio **disowns** his daughter.
- Iago **convinces** Roderigo to **raise more money**, telling him that it will help him win Desdemona's **love**.
- In a **soliloquy**, Iago **plans** to get **revenge** on Othello by **convincing** him that his wife is **unfaithful**.

In this scene, there are **hints** about what will **happen later** in the play:

1) Brabantio's **final words** are a **warning** to Othello: "**She has deceived her father, and may thee**" (line 290). This **anticipates** the fact that Othello will become **convinced** of Desdemona's **deception** even though she **remains loyal**. Iago echoes this line in **Act 3, Scene 3**: "**She did deceive her father, marrying you**" (3.3.204).

2) Othello's response to Brabantio, "**My life upon her faith!**" (line 291), is later shown to be **ironic**. He **bets his life** that Desdemona is **faithful** to him but it **costs** them **both** their **lives** when he starts to **doubt** her.

Shakespeare *Explores* Othello and Desdemona's *Relationship*

Different characters voice their **varying opinions** about the **marriage**:

1) Brabantio continues to be **critical** of the **marriage** and **forces** Desdemona to **choose** between himself and Othello. Brabantio sees Desdemona as his **property** — he describes her as a "**jewel**" (line 193). He also **echoes** Iago's accusation that Othello is a **thief** by claiming that she has been "**stolen**" (line 60) from him.

© Johan Persson / ArenaPAL

2) Othello and Desdemona **defend** their relationship **against claims** that it's **unnatural** or **immoral**. Together they prove that Desdemona was "**half the wooer**" (line 174) and that their **relationship** is **based on equal affection** rather than **lust**. Desdemona pledges her "**duty**" (line 184) to Othello, but she also has a **say** in their **relationship** e.g. she **demands** to be **allowed** to go with Othello to **Cyprus**.

3) Iago is **disdainful** of Othello and Desdemona's relationship — he tells Roderigo that the only things keeping them together are "**sanctimony and a frail vow**" (line 350). Iago also accuses the couple of being **fickle** — he says that "**These Moors are changeable in their wills**" (lines 342-343) and that Desdemona "**must change for youth**" (lines 345-346). He doesn't believe that their love can **last**.

Sanctimony means false devotion.

4) The Duke says "**I think this tale would win my daughter too**" (line 170) — he **supports** their **marriage** and **defends** Othello against Brabantio's racism, calling him "**Valiant**" and "**fair**" (lines 48 and 287).

The word Moor was often applied to people from the Barbary coast in North Africa — many critics argue that this was where Othello was supposed to have originated from.

Racism Exists *in* Venetian Society

This scene demonstrates that there is **racism** in Venetian society:

1) Iago describes Othello as a "**barbarian**" (line 351). This could refer to **where** Othello is **from**, but it also suggests **savagery**. It links to Iago's comparison of Othello with a "**Barbary horse**" (1.1.112) where he jokes that Brabantio's descendents will be horses — "**coursers**" and "**jennets**" (1.1.113-114).

2) Brabantio thinks Desdemona should have "**feared to look on**" Othello (line 98) because of his race, and their love is "**Against all rules of nature**" (line 101). He believes that only the "**practices of cunning hell**" (line 102) would convince a **white woman** to fall in **love** with a **black man**. However, the only "**witchcraft**" (line 64) Othello used was to tell the story of his life. This **challenges** the **stereotypes** that would have been held by Shakespeare's **audience**.

3) In Elizabethan times, blackness was associated with evil — later in the play Emilia calls Othello "**the blacker devil!**" (5.2.132). However, in this scene, the Duke **praises** Othello by saying that he's "**far more fair than black**" (line 287). He **highlights** Othello's **nobility** to show that Brabantio's **racial prejudices** are **unjustified** (see p.24).

Act 1, Scene 3

Othello *Tries* to *Separate* the *Roles* of *Husband* and *Soldier*

The scene begins with a discussion of **military matters**, which establishes the **masculine backdrop** of **war**:

1) Before Othello marries Desdemona, his **identity** as a **soldier** is **clear**, and he **defines himself** through his **military successes**. This is **evident** when he claims that he is "**Rude**" (line 81) in **speech** because he has spent so much time "**in the tented field**" of war (line 85).

2) Because of this, his **reputation** is **very important** to him. A **senator**, the **Duke** and **Desdemona** all describe him as being "**valiant**" (lines 47, 48 and 250) and he's keen to **maintain** this **impression**.

3) It's implied in this scene that Othello is **worried** that his **role** as a **husband** might **affect** his **military abilities** — this is why he is so **keen** to **play down** any **sexual attraction** for Desdemona: "**I therefore beg it not / To please the palate of my appetite**" (lines 258-259). He claims that if his **love** for Desdemona should **interfere** with military matters then they should "**Let housewives make a skillet of my helm**" (line 269).

However, Othello cannot **separate** his roles as husband and soldier — the two have **already** become **intertwined** in the couple's **courtship**. It was Othello's **tales of war** that **attracted** Desdemona to him in the first place, as she did "**Devour**" (line 149) them with a "**greedy ear**" (line 148). Desdemona makes Othello **feel heroic** because she **values** his **identity** as a **soldier** — it's one of the reasons he loves her. She wants to be **part** of his **military career**, requesting to go with him to Cyprus and refusing to be a "**moth of peace**" (line 253).

Iago develops his *Evil Plot*

Early in the play, Iago often has soliloquies — this gives the audience an insight into the way his plan develops.

Through Iago's **soliloquy**, Shakespeare **anticipates** his **increasingly evil** plans:

1) In this scene, Iago suggests **various motives** for his **plotting** — he suggests that he's **jealous** of **Cassio**, and he **suspects** that **Othello** has slept with **Emilia**: "'twixt my sheets / He's done my office" (lines 381-382). However, Iago also seems to plot for his own **amusement**, and calls it "**sport**" (lines 364 and 380).

2) Shakespeare demonstrates that Iago is **skilled** at **thinking on his feet**, by showing that Iago is working out his plan **while he speaks** — he uses phrases like "**let me see now**" (line 386) and "**How? How? Let's see**" (line 388). This hints at his **ability** to **take advantage** of situations and **improvise**.

3) In his **conversation** with Roderigo, Iago refers to the **formation** of his **plan** as a **birth**: "**There are many events in the womb of time, which will be delivered**" (lines 364-365). In his soliloquy, Iago describes his plan as something that is "**engendered**" (line 397) (**conceived**) and talks about its "**monstrous birth**" (line 398). Iago **twists** the **language** of **birth** and **new life** to talk about something **deathly** — what will be "**delivered**" (line 365) won't be **positive**, but instead will be a **plan** for **death and destruction**.

4) The idea of the "**monstrous birth**" links to Iago's **hellish language** — he talks about "**Hell and night**" (line 397), and he says he will use "**all the tribe of hell**" (line 352), which **associates** Iago with **dark forces**. This shows how completely Iago **contrasts** with Othello, who Iago **admits** is of a "**free and open nature**" (line 393).

5) According to Iago, Othello "**thinks men honest that but seem to be so**" (line 394). This links back to Othello's last speech where he calls Iago "**Honest**" (line 291). Iago reveals that he intends to **take advantage** of Othello's **trusting nature** — he compares men like Othello to "**asses**" (line 396) because they are so **easily led**. This is another example of Iago using **animalistic language** to **dehumanise** Othello.

Practice Questions

Q1 'Brabantio's objections to Othello and Desdemona's marriage stem purely from racism.' To what extent do you agree with this statement? Back up your answer with examples from the text.

Q2 What effect do you think Act 1 has on the audience? How would *Othello* be different without Act 1?

"She has deceived her father, and may thee"

I can't believe Othello got Desdemona by just telling her some boring war stories — it's so crazy it might just work. Yeah... tell your date the story of your whole life up till now. People love it when you just won't stop talking about yourself. Good advice Shakey.

Act 2, Scene 1

The rest of the play is set on the island of Cyprus. This scene opens as the Venetian ships arrive...

The **Action** moves to **Cyprus**...

- A **storm** has destroyed the **Turkish fleet** and **separated** the Venetian ships.
- **Cassio's ship** arrives in Cyprus **first**, then Iago and Desdemona join him. They **wait** for **Othello**.
- Othello's ship **finally** arrives and Desdemona is very **relieved**. They prepare a **celebration**.
- **Iago** suggests **further motives** for his plan to **destroy Othello, Desdemona** and **Cassio**.

The change in **setting** isn't just a change in **location** — it's also a **symbolic transition**:

1) The main characters travel from their **homes** in **peaceful** and **civilised** Venice, to an **unfamiliar**, "**warlike isle**" (line 43). Cyprus is a place of **conflict** and **disorder**.

2) The characters are more **isolated** in Cyprus which means that Iago can prey on their **weaknesses** more easily. The **island setting** also gives the rest of *Othello* a **claustrophobic** feeling — the characters are **trapped**.

The **Storm** is important to the **Plot**

1) The storm is significant because it quickly gets rid of the **threat of war** by destroying the Turkish fleet. This is an example of '**deus ex machina**' — the threat of war **conveniently moves** the main characters to Cyprus and the destruction of the **fleet** allows the play to **focus solely** on the **disintegration** of Othello and Desdemona's **marriage**.

> The term 'deus ex machina' is used to describe an unrealistic plot device that resolves problems in the plot.

2) The storm also foreshadows the **events** of the rest of the play:

- Cassio says that **Iago** had "**most favourable and happy speed**" (line 67) on his journey, **despite** the storm. This gives the audience an **indication** that things are **going well** for Iago, and that his plot may **succeed**.
- Shakespeare tells the audience **twice** that the ships carrying Othello and Cassio were "**parted**" (line 33) by the **storm**. This **anticipates** that soon they will be divided **permanently** by Iago's **scheming**.
- Othello tells Desdemona that "**If after every tempest come such calms / May the winds blow till they have wakened death**" (lines 179-180). This image is **prophetic** — a greater 'storm' is about to hit their relationship as **Iago** puts his plan into action. This line also hints that **death** will be "**wakened**" by the end of the play.

> Othello often uses sea imagery to describe their marriage.

Shakespeare **Reveals** more about the **Characters** in this scene

Cassio
In this scene, **Cassio** comes across as **polite** and **gallant** — he praises Desdemona, describing her as "**divine**" (line 73) and says that she "**paragons description and wild fame**" (line 62). He also "*kisses Emilia*" (between lines 99 and 100). **Iago** will **use** these characteristics to convince Othello that Cassio loves **Desdemona**.

Desdemona
Iago and Desdemona's **conversation** between lines 100 and 164 shows **Desdemona in a new light**. She **understands** Iago's **sexual innuendo** and shows that she can be **flirtatious**, asking Iago "**how wouldst thou praise me?**" (line 123). This suggests that she isn't an innocent "**maid, so tender**" (1.2.66) who's "**never bold**" (1.3.94).

Iago
This scene reinforces Iago's status as the play's **villain**. His conversation with Desdemona and Emilia is full of **misogyny**, with lines like "**You rise to play and go to bed to work**" (line 114). Iago's **soliloquy** also reveals that he's **skilled** at finding a person's **weakness** and using it against them — he **commands Roderigo** by using his **love** for Desdemona, "**sir, be you ruled by me**" (line 255), and he plans to manipulate Cassio by using his courtesy and "**choler**" (line 263) against him: "**With as little a web as this will I ensnare as great a fly as Cassio**" (lines 165-166).

Othello
Othello's **excesses of emotion** are clear after his arrival in Cyprus — he says he's "**most happy**" and his "**soul hath her content so absolute**" (lines 184-185). These strong feelings hint that his **negative emotions** will also be **intense** and **destructive** — Iago vows to "**put the Moor / At least into a jealousy so strong / That judgement cannot cure**" (lines 291-293).

> Jealousy plays an important role in both Othello's downfall, and Iago's motivations.

Act 2, Scenes 1-2

Othello and Desdemona are **Deeply** in **Love**

© Johan Persson / ArenaPAL

1) Othello's **reunion** with Desdemona highlights their **mutual love** and **affection**. They even **finish** each other's **lines**, which demonstrates how **close** they have become. Desdemona calls him "**My dear Othello**" (line 176) and he calls her his "**soul's joy**" (line 178) which **elevates** their love to having **spiritual significance**.

> In an aside, Iago observes that the lovers are "**well tuned now**" (line 193) but vows to "**set down the pegs that make this music**" (line 194) — pegs are used to loosen the strings on **stringed instruments** so they're **out of tune**. Iago plans to manipulate events in order to **upset their happiness**.

2) Othello highlights the **equality** in their **relationship** by calling Desdemona "**my fair warrior**" (line 176). By calling her a "**warrior**" Othello associates her with his **own military role** and **recognises** that she's put herself in **danger** by taking part in the **masculine affair** of **war**.

Iago's **Motivation isn't Clear**

1) In his **soliloquy** at the end of the scene, Iago gives **three reasons** for his plots **against** Othello, Desdemona and Cassio:

Othello's slept with Emilia	**He's in love with Desdemona**	**Cassio's slept with Emilia**
He repeats his accusation that Othello has had an **affair** with Emilia. He proclaims that "**nothing can, or shall, content my soul**" (line 289) until he has had **revenge**.	Iago declares that he loves Desdemona — "**Now, I do love her too**" (line 282) but he says that this is partly "**to diet my revenge**" (line 285).	He also suggests that **Cassio** may have slept with Emilia too — "**I fear Cassio with my night-cap too**" (line 298).

2) Even when he's **alone** on stage, Iago's **motivations** aren't consistent, though here he suggests that he's motivated by **jealousy**. Throughout the play Iago **compares jealousy** to a 'poison' — in this scene, he claims that it "**Doth, like a poisonous mineral, gnaw my inwards**" (line 288) which presents it as **destructive** and **unnatural**.

3) The fact that he doesn't seem to have a **single reason** for his **plotting**, and his admission that his plans are "**confused**" (line 302), could suggest that he's simply **creating disorder** because he's **evil**.

Act 2, Scene 2 — A **Herald** announces a **Celebration**...

• A **herald** reads a **proclamation** — the city will **celebrate** their military **victory** and Othello's **marriage**.

This **short scene** establishes the **peace** on Cyprus. However, it also **creates** a **mood** of **anticipation**.

1) This scene **contrasts** with Iago's soliloquy at the end of the previous scene — it **suggests** that the whole island is **rejoicing** in their victory, but the **audience** is left with a sense of **foreboding** as they wonder how Iago's plans will **develop** during the celebrations.

2) The herald announces a **celebration** of the **new marriage** and the **military triumph** which suggests that it's possible to combine matters of **love** and **war**. However, the **violent interruption** of the **wedding celebrations** in **Act 2, Scene 3** suggests otherwise.

> This celebration is ironic, because the audience would have known that the Venetians' victory in Cyprus was short-lived, much like Othello and Desdemona's marriage (see p.55).

Practice Questions

Q1 Compare and contrast Iago's soliloquy at the end of Act 2, Scene 1 with his soliloquy at the end of Act 1, Scene 3.

Q2 What evidence is there in Act 2, Scenes 1-2, that suggests there is trouble ahead for Othello and Desdemona?

"I'll set down the pegs that make this music"

Something tells me Iago's music isn't going to be harmonious — no doubt it'll be full of discords. In fact, he's an awful musician, he once mistook a flute for a sophisticated long-range pea shooter, and thought that you found a tempo on the side of your head.

Act 2, Scene 3

Cyprus celebrates the destruction of the Turkish fleet. Meanwhile, Iago puts his plot against Cassio into action...

The **Celebrations** are **Interrupted** by a **Fight**...

- Othello leaves Cassio to **keep order** on the island as he and Desdemona go to **consummate** their marriage.
- Iago **tries** to make Cassio admit that he has **feelings** for Desdemona. When he fails, he **gets him drunk** instead.
- Acting on **Iago's instructions**, Roderigo provokes Cassio who **chases** him. Montano stops Cassio and they **fight**.
- Cassio **wounds Montano**, just as Othello enters. **Iago** gives **his version** of events so that Othello **fires Cassio**.
- Iago **advises** Cassio to try to convince Desdemona to help him **regain** his position as Othello's lieutenant.

Shakespeare uses several **dramatic features** which make this scene **stand out** from the rest of Act 2:

1) After the **uninterrupted dialogue** of the previous scenes, Act 2, Scene 3 provides some **action**.
   The fight is **sudden** and **shocking**, with shouting and alarm bells in the middle of the night.

2) This commotion is brought to a sudden halt by **Othello's entrance**. He restores order, but is initially **furious**
   with those involved. His usually flowing speech is **broken up** into shorter sentences and questions — he asks
   "**Why, how now, ho! From whence ariseth this?**" (line 163). His questions show his **anger** and **frustration**.

3) There are many entrances and exits in this scene, but **Iago** is almost a **constant** presence on stage.
   His **three soliloquies** leave the audience with the impression that he is in **total control** of the unfolding events.

The **Fight Ruins** Othello and Desdemona's **Reunion**

The fight is **significant** because it **interrupts** the **only time** that Othello and Desdemona have **been alone** in the play:

1) Othello's **language** at the **beginning** of this scene suggests that they're leaving to **consummate** their **marriage**:
   "**the fruits are to ensue: / That profit's yet to come 'tween me and you**" (lines 9-10). This **undermines** Iago's
   earlier **insinuations** that their marriage is based on **bestial sexual desires** as they haven't yet **consummated** it.

2) The fight **interrupts** their **union** as Othello returns to **restore order**. Some critics, such as Harold Bloom
   (see p.29) have suggested that Othello **leaves Desdemona before** they have **consummated** their **marriage** —
   Bloom argues that this adds to the **tragedy** of the play because they weren't able to **celebrate** their **love**.

3) In **Act 1, Scene 3** Othello promised that he would keep **love** and **war** separate, but here their love is **interrupted**
   by **conflict**: "**'tis the soldiers' life / To have their balmy slumbers waked with strife**" (lines 250-251). This
   foreshadows the **future problems** in Desdemona and Othello's relationship. Iago also says, "**Our General's wife is
   now the General**" (lines 305-306) which suggests that the **boundaries** between the **two worlds** are starting to **blur**.

4) However, the couple still seem happy here — the way that Othello **tenderly** takes Desdemona **back to bed** in this
   scene starkly contrasts with the way he **orders** her to bed in **Act 4, Scene 3** (line 7) when he's about to **murder her**.

Iago's **Methods** start to become **Clear**

In this scene, Iago reveals his ability to identify a person's **weakness** and **use** it against them:

| Desdemona | Her goodness becomes a weakness that Iago can use — "**So will I turn her virtue into pitch**" (line 350). |

| Cassio | He gets drunk easily — "**If I can fasten but one cup upon him**" (line 44). |

| Roderigo | His love for Desdemona has made him a "**sick fool**" (line 47), which Iago uses to convince him to fight. |

| Emilia | Her unwavering devotion to Iago means he can **control** her actions — "**I'll set her on**" (line 373). |

Iago continues to develop the **imagery** of his **plotting**:

- He compares his plot to a "**net / That shall enmesh them all**" (lines 351-352), and describes Othello's soul as
  "**enfettered**" (line 335) to love. These images of **entrapment** suggest that nobody can **escape** from his plots.
- Again, Iago **associates** his **words** with **poison** — he plans to pour the "**pestilence**" (line 346) of **suspicion** into
  Othello's ear, which links to Act 3, Scene 3 where he claims "**The Moor already changes with my poison**" (3.3.322).

Act 3, Scenes 1-2

These two scenes show the aftermath of Cassio's fight, and prepare the audience for Act 3, Scene 3...

Act 3, Scene 1 — *Cassio tries to* **Win Back** *Othello's* **Favour***...*

- **Cassio** arranges for some **musicians** to play to Othello and Desdemona, but Othello **pays** them to **leave**.
- **Emilia** agrees to help Cassio talk to **Desdemona**. He hopes that Desdemona will **defend him** to Othello.

This short scene provides some **light-hearted comedy** before the **focus** shifts back to Iago's main plot:

1) The clown's teasing of the musicians provides some **comic relief** after Cassio's **anguish** and Iago's relentless **scheming** in Act 2, Scene 3. Their dialogue contains **sexual puns** on the word "**tail**" (lines 8-9) which would have appealed to an **Elizabethan audience**. However, the comic interlude is **short-lived** as Cassio sends the clown to find Emilia, and the action returns to **Iago's plots**.

2) When Iago offers to distract Othello so that Cassio can talk to Desdemona, Cassio comments that he "**never knew a Florentine more kind and honest**" than Iago (line 39). This shows that Iago's **power** lies in the fact that he is **trusted** by the other characters who **fail** to see his **true nature**.

3) Cassio asks Emilia to arrange for him to talk to Desdemona "**alone**" (line 52). Shakespeare uses **dramatic irony** to great effect in this scene — the audience **knows** that Iago will use the meeting between Cassio and Desdemona to **convince Othello** that they are having an affair. Iago's "**net**" (2.3.351) is already closing around the characters.

Act 3, Scene 2 — *Othello turns to* **Military Matters***...*

- Othello asks Iago to pay his **respects** to the council and then joins him as he **inspects** the island's **fortifications**.

This brief scene continues to **build up** to the **pivotal** scene of the play — **Act 3, Scene 3**.

1) This scene adds to the **dramatic irony** — the audience knows that Iago wanted to "**draw the Moor apart**" (2.3.374) to give Cassio a chance to plead with Desdemona. This seems to be the **perfect opportunity** as Othello is **distracted** by work — events still seem to be **going Iago's way**.

2) In Act 1, Scene 3, Othello emphatically **denies** that his marriage will make him **neglect** the "**serious and great business**" (1.3.264) of his military duties. **Ironically**, though, his **military business** causes him to **leave** his wife in this scene, which allows Iago's **malicious plan** to progress further.

> Othello's **inspection** of the fortifications **reminds** the audience of his **role** as a **leader** and a **soldier**, but it's also the **last** time the war is mentioned in the play. The **focus** of the play now moves away from the **war** onto Othello and Desdemona's **marriage**. This adds to the sense of **scrutiny** that has surrounded their relationship since **Act 1, Scene 1**.

Practice Questions

Q1 'If Cassio had remained sober, Iago's plan would not have been successful.'
Using Act 2, Scene 3 as a starting point, to what extent do you agree with this statement?

Q2 Many critics have argued that there is an underlying conflict throughout *Othello* between public and private life. Assess how this conflict is presented in these three scenes? How important do you think the conflict is to the play as a whole?

Q3 'The appointment of Cassio, a drunk, as his lieutenant shows a lack of judgement on Othello's part.'
With reference to Act 2, Scene 3 and Act 3, Scene 1, how far do you agree with this statement?

"If consequence do but approve my dream / My boat sails freely"

I don't like Iago much, but he definitely does make things a bit more interesting. Iago may be one of the most hateful characters ever written, but imagine how dull the play would have been without Iago's plotting to jazz it up a bit. Yep — really, really dull.

Act 3, Scene 3

Cassio asks Desdemona to help him get his job back, but he quickly leaves when he sees Othello coming...

Iago **Persuades Othello** that Desdemona is **Unfaithful**...

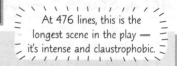
At 476 lines, this is the longest scene in the play — it's intense and claustrophobic.

- Desdemona kindly agrees to talk to Othello on **Cassio's behalf**. She **begs** Othello to reinstate Cassio as his **lieutenant**, but Othello asks her to **leave**.
- Once Iago and Othello are **alone**, Iago starts to **persuade** Othello that Desdemona is **unfaithful**. Desdemona returns and thinks that Othello looks **unwell**. She tries to **nurse** him, and drops her **handkerchief**.
- Emilia takes the handkerchief and gives it to **Iago**. Iago plans to **plant** it in **Cassio's lodgings**.
- Iago's stories **convince** Othello of the affair, and he asks Iago to **kill Cassio**. Othello plans to **kill Desdemona**.

This scene is a **turning point** for Othello as Iago persuades him to **give in completely** to jealousy:

1) Iago uses **relentless persuasive techniques** in this scene. In the opening lines, Othello seems to have no **suspicions** about Desdemona's fidelity, but by the end, Iago has **convinced** him that she has been unfaithful.

2) The scene is full of **entrances** and **exits**, which create **confusion**. **Iago** is the only **constant** — he is on stage for the **entire** scene, with the exception of lines 254 to 296. This allows him to **take advantage** of Othello's **turmoil**.

3) Even when Iago is off stage, the characters still **talk** about him — Othello describes him as a man "**of exceeding honesty**" (line 255) and Emilia plans to give him the **handkerchief** as soon as she sees him, because he "**hath a hundred times / Wooed [her] to steal it**" (lines 289-290). This shows that Iago remains **in control** of the entire scene.

Iago and Desdemona use **Different Methods** to **Persuade** Othello

1) In this scene, Shakespeare creates a **contrast** between the **honest** and **selfless** Desdemona, and the **dishonest** and **self-serving** Iago. In comparison with Iago, **Desdemona's** persuasion of Othello is **sincere** and **simple**:

> **Desdemona**
> - Desdemona tries to persuade Othello to **reinstate Cassio** by **simply asking** him to. She **doesn't try** to **manipulate** her husband, but speaks with **urgency**, appealing to him with her "**grace or power**" (line 46).
> - She **compares** her insistent appeals for Cassio's **reinstatement** to asking Othello to "**wear your gloves / Or feed on nourishing dishes**" (lines 77-78) — she **emphasises** that she's acting in Othello's **best interests**, and links this to the **domestic concerns** of a **dutiful** and "**obedient**" wife (line 89).
> - Her language could be seen as **nagging**, as she repeatedly presses Othello to meet Cassio: "**Why, then, tomorrow night, or Tuesday morn, / On Tuesday noon, or night; on Wednesday morn**" (lines 60-61). Desdemona's **persistence** leads Othello to suspect that she has a **hidden motive** — that she **loves Cassio**.

2) Othello seems reluctant to listen to his wife, and gives vague answers before dismissing her: "**Prithee, no more: let him come when he will**" (line 75). However, the fact that Othello tells Desdemona that he "**will deny [her] nothing**" (line 83) suggests that she can still **influence** him.

3) The passage between lines 90 and 254 is the **first** time in the play that Othello and Iago are **alone** on stage together. Iago takes **full advantage** of the **opportunity** to influence Othello's thoughts:

Iago's reluctance to speak foreshadows his refusal to explain his motives in Act 5, Scene 2.

> **Iago**
> - Unlike Desdemona, Iago feigns **reluctance** to speak, which makes Othello **curious**: "**I prithee speak to me**" (line 130). Iago lets Othello draw his **own** conclusions: "**It were not for your quiet... To let you know my thoughts**" (lines 151-153). This makes Othello suspect his wife is guilty of **more** than Iago says: "**This honest creature doubtless / Sees and knows more... than he unfolds**" (lines 240-241).
> - Iago uses **leading questions** such as "**Did Michael Cassio... know of your love?**" (lines 93-94) to imply that Othello should be **suspicious** of Cassio and Desdemona. By **involving** Othello in his 'thought process', Iago makes it seem as if the **idea** of Desdemona's infidelity has come from **Othello himself**.
> - Iago **warns** Othello that Desdemona "**did deceive her father, marrying you**" (line 204), **echoing** Brabantio's warning in Act 1, Scene 3. He uses her decision to **marry Othello** as a reason to **distrust** her.
> - Iago **uses** Desdemona's **kindness against** her — he sees how eager she is to support Cassio, and **corrupts** Othello's mind so that the more she **presses** Othello, the more he believes that she has **betrayed** him.
> - Iago only provides **specific details**, such as Cassio's 'dream', when Othello **demands** them. His **reluctance** to speak, and his **precise details**, make his stories sound **credible** despite their implausibility.

Act 3, Scene 3

Honesty is a Major Theme in this scene

For more on honesty and deception, see p.43.

© Johan Persson / ArenaPAL

1) **Honesty** is important in *Othello* — the words '**honest**' and '**honesty**' are used **twenty times** in this scene alone. 'Honesty' is related to **truthfulness**, **integrity** and, in women, **chastity**.

2) A key reason for Iago's **success** in manipulating Othello is that he is **perceived** as a man of "**exceeding honesty**" (line 255). It's **ironic** that Othello believes Iago is **truthful** when he accuses Desdemona of **dishonesty** and Cassio of lacking **integrity**.

3) Othello's **confusion** is highlighted when he tells Iago "**I think my wife be honest, and think she is not; / I think that thou art just, and think thou art not**" (lines 381-382). His **indecision** shows that he is no longer able to tell **reality** from **appearance**.

4) The word 'honest' was also associated with a **lack of sophistication**. Iago is often called honest, implying he's **socially inferior** — his **resentment** may help to explain his actions.

Iago starts to Replace Desdemona in Othello's Affections

1) As Othello starts to **doubt** and **suspect** Desdemona, Iago increasingly **takes her place** in Othello's mind. Iago's **ascent** to **power** over Othello is in **direct parallel** with Desdemona's **downfall**.

2) The change takes place over the course of this scene. In the **middle** of Act 3, Scene 3, Othello still maintains that "**If [Desdemona] be false... / I'll not believe't**" (line 275). However, when he **returns** to the **stage** at line 326, he demands that Iago "**prove my love a whore**" (line 356) — he has come to **trust Iago** more than his **wife**.

3) Iago's **influence** over Othello is evident in Othello's **changing language**. In previous scenes, Othello's language is **measured** and **controlled**, but in this scene it begins to **deteriorate** and reflect Iago's own **vocabulary**:

- Othello's previous **eloquent** and **lengthy** speeches become **short exclamations** like "**O misery!**" (line 169). In this scene, Othello allows Iago to make **longer speeches** which shows that **Iago** is becoming more **dominant**.

- Othello's words and thoughts also begin to **mirror** Iago's. For example, Othello adopts Iago's **misogynistic** views, referring to Desdemona as "**lewd minx**" and "**fair devil**" (lines 472-475). His **language** becomes **violent**: "**I'll tear her all to pieces!**" (line 428), and he begins to **curse**: "**O, damn her, damn her!**" (line 472), which echoes Iago's **coarse** language and references to **hell**.

- Othello claims that Desdemona's "**name that was as fresh / As Dian's visage is now begrimed and black / As mine own face**" (lines 383-385). This shows that he sees her as **corrupted** and **blackened** and hints that he has **absorbed** Iago's **racist** ideas.

  Diana was the Roman goddess of the moon, and of chastity.

4) At the end of Act 3, Scene 3, Othello **kneels** in front of Iago, demonstrating to the audience how **powerful** Iago has become. Iago then kneels down and they **pledge loyalty** to each other in a **parody** of an Elizabethan wedding ceremony. Iago calls on the stars to "**Witness**" (line 460) him giving himself to Othello's service and his final line, "**I am your own for ever**" (line 477) mirrors Othello's earlier words — "**I am bound to thee for ever**" (line 211).

Shakespeare develops the Theme of Jealousy

For more on jealousy, see p.36-37.

1) Some critics have taken Othello's **rapid** acceptance of Iago's stories as **evidence** that he is **predisposed** to **jealousy**. Othello's **insecurities** make him **susceptible** to Iago's suggestions — it's **Othello** who first mentions **race**, describing **Desdemona's choice** as "**nature erring from itself**" (line 225). Iago **encourages** this idea and suggests that Desdemona may **compare** Othello to her "**country forms, / And happily repent**" their marriage (lines 235-236).

2) In this scene, Shakespeare introduces the idea that **jealousy** is like **poison**:

- Iago compares jealousy to "**poisons**" which, with manipulation, "**Burn like the mines of sulphur**" (lines 323-326). He suggests that once jealous thoughts have been **planted**, they are very difficult to get rid of.

  The "mines of sulphur" is a euphemism for hell, continuing the motif of damnation that runs through the play.

- Othello calls on **hate** to replace **love** in his heart, and acknowledges that his **heart** is "**of aspics' tongues**" (line 447). An **asp** is a **venomous snake** — Othello's **heart** is full of **poison**.

3) Shakespeare also introduces the idea of jealousy as a "**monster**" (line 106), implying that it is **unnatural** and **evil**. This is reflected in the portrayal of jealousy as **all-consuming** — Othello is "**eaten up**" (line 388) by it.

Act 3, Scene 3

The **Handkerchief** symbolises **Love** and **Betrayal**

1) The handkerchief was Desdemona's "**first remembrance**" from Othello (line 288) so it represents their **relationship** and her **loyalty** to him. When she **loses** it, Othello believes she has also lost her **chastity**.

2) Ironically, Othello is **partially responsible** for the loss of the handkerchief — when Desdemona drops it he tells her to "**Let it alone**" (line 285). Emilia gives it to **Iago**, which eventually leads to the newlyweds' **downfall**.

3) It's **ominous** that Iago has asked Emilia to steal the handkerchief "**a hundred times**" (line 289). The audience suspects that Iago has a cunning plan for it, and a few lines later he reveals that he will plant it "**in Cassio's lodging**" (line 318).

4) Iago recognises that "**Trifles light as air / Are to the jealous confirmations strong / As proofs of holy writ**" (lines 319-321). Iago sees that if he makes Othello **jealous** enough, Othello will accept Cassio's possession of the **handkerchief** as the "**ocular proof**" (line 357) he needs to believe that Desdemona is **unfaithful**.

> ### Women and the Handkerchief
> Emilia takes the handkerchief for Iago, saying "**I nothing, but to please his fantasy**" (line 296). This shows that she believes her role is to **please** her husband, even though he **treats her badly**. **Desdemona** also feels a "**duty**" (1.3.182) to her **husband**, saying "**Whate'er you be, I am obedient**" (line 89).

Othello becomes **Increasingly Irrational**

1) There's a **brief pause** in Iago's persuasion when Othello **leaves the stage** at line 286. When Othello returns, his **calmness** has vanished, and he's increasingly **emotional**. He imagines "**Cassio's kisses on [Desdemona's] lips**" (line 338) and the "**general camp**" enjoying "**her sweet body**" (lines 342-343). The audience sees that Othello's prediction that when his love for Desdemona fails, "**Chaos is come again**" (line 92) is starting to come true.

2) Othello's loss of **rationality** allows Iago to move away from **implications** to using **crude language** more openly. He graphically describes Cassio and Desdemona using **animal imagery** — "**as prime as goats, as hot as monkeys, / As salt as wolves in pride**" (lines 400-401).

> The words 'prime', 'hot', 'salt' and 'in pride' can be used to describe animals at times when they're most sexually active.

3) Othello seems to **abandon reason** in this scene — he claims to want "**ocular proof**" (line 357) of Desdemona's infidelity, but is easily **convinced** by Iago's report of Cassio's dream. He also believes **without hesitation** that Iago saw Cassio "**wipe his beard**" (line 436) with the handkerchief.

4) Othello's **language** reflects his loss of **self-control**. His lines are **short** and **violent**, for example "**I'll tear her all to pieces!**" (line 428) and "**O, blood, blood, blood!**" (line 448), showing that his **anger** has **taken over**.

By the **End** of Act 3, Scene 3, the play's **Tragic Ending** is **Inevitable**

1) Othello **initially** says that if Desdemona is **unfaithful**, he will "**whistle her off, and let her down the wind / To prey at fortune**" (lines 259-260) — at this point he only plans to **separate** from her. However, by the **end** of the scene, Othello has decided that she must **die** — he leaves to find "**some swift means of death**" (line 474) for her.

2) The audience can now identify Othello as a **tragic hero**, according to **Aristotle's theory** (see p.46). It could be argued that Othello's **jealousy** becomes his **tragic flaw** — both he and Desdemona will **die** as a result of it.

3) Shakespeare uses images of the **sea** to increase the feeling of **inevitability**:

> - Othello compares himself to an **ocean current** whose "**compulsive course**" (line 451) is **unstoppable**.
> - He compares his feelings to the tide, showing that love is in retreat. He says that he "**Shall ne'er look back, ne'er ebb to humble love**" (line 455).

> Previously Othello used maritime language to refer to his and Desdemona's marriage (see p.10).

4) In this scene, Othello's roles as **soldier** and **husband** are in **conflict**. He believes that Desdemona's infidelity has destroyed his **career**: "**Othello's occupation's gone**" (line 354). Faced with losing everything, his **military** side eventually takes over and he **regains control**. His early **confusion** is replaced with a **conviction** that he **must act** and kill Desdemona.

© Nigel Norrington / ArenaPAL

Act 3, Scene 4

Desdemona starts worrying about her lost handkerchief just as Othello comes looking for it...

Iago's **Plan** starts to produce **Results**...

- Desdemona makes Othello **angry** by asking him **once again** to **reinstate Cassio**.
- Othello asks to borrow her **handkerchief** and gets even **angrier** when she can't produce it.
- Emilia suggests that Othello is **jealous**, but Desdemona thinks it must be **something else**.
- Cassio gives the **handkerchief** to **Bianca** and asks her to make a copy of it. She thinks it's from **another woman**.

Act 3, Scene 3 and Act 4, Scene 1 both **focus** on **Othello**, but the focus of Act 3, Scene 4 changes to **Desdemona**.

1) During this scene, Desdemona **realises** that something has come between herself and Othello. She sees that her "**advocation is not now in tune**" (line 119) which indicates a shift from Iago's earlier observation that they are "**well tuned**" (2.1.193). He has already **succeeded** in destroying the **harmony** of their relationship.

2) Iago **only speaks three times** in the whole scene. Although he says little, he still **controls** events — having planted **doubts** in Othello's mind, he sits back and watches the results. His **repeated question** about whether Othello is "**angry**" (lines 128 and 130) reveals his **delight** at how well his plan is going.

Othello becomes **Obsessed** with the **Handkerchief**

The word "web" links the handkerchief to the "web" (2.1.165) of Iago's plot. The handkerchief is now the most vital part of Iago's plan to convince Othello of Desdemona's infidelity.

1) The **handkerchief** seems to possess almost **magical properties** for Othello:

- He claims that "**there's magic in the web of it**" (line 69).
- His claim that its owner will be able to "**subdue**" her partner "**Entirely to her love**" (lines 59-60), could suggest that Othello is starting to suspect that Desdemona **tricked** him into loving her. This **reverses** the roles that Brabantio suggested, where Desdemona was the **victim** of Othello's **witchcraft**.
- The use of **language** associated with **magic**, such as "**sibyl**" and "**prophetic**" (lines 70-72) emphasises the handkerchief's **importance** and **power**, both to Othello and in the **events** of the play.

'Perdition' means damnation or ruin.

2) In Act 3, Scene 3, Othello declares: "**Perdition catch my soul / But I do love thee!**" (3.3.90-91), meaning that he would be **damned** if he stopped loving her. In this scene, the **loss** of the **handkerchief** would bring about "**perdition**" (line 67) for **Desdemona** — this shows how **important** it is to Othello.

The **Women** in the play **Contrast** with each other

For more on gender and sexuality, see p.38-9.

All three women in *Othello* appear in this scene so their **differences** are **emphasised**:

Emilia	Desdemona	Bianca
Emilia is **cynical** about men, **worldly** enough to realise that Othello is **jealous** and knows that jealous people "**are not ever jealous**" for a "**cause**" (line 156).	Desdemona appears **innocent** and **naive** in this scene. She ignores Emilia's **warnings** about Othello's **jealousy**, and simply **hopes** that it's state business that has "**puddled his clear spirit**" (line 139).	As a courtesan, Bianca is a **foil** to Desdemona (see p.33). Despite her **independent profession**, she is **submissive** to men, just like the other women. She **obeys** Cassio when he sends her away — "**I must be circumstanced**" (line 197).

Regardless of their **class** or **profession**, all three women are treated **badly** by **male** characters, and especially their **lovers**.

Practice Questions

Q1 With reference to Act 3, Scene 3, to what extent is Emilia responsible for the tragic ending of the play?

Q2 By looking at Act 3, Scenes 3 and 4, assess how the symbolism of the handkerchief changes for Othello.

"To lose or give't away were such perdition / As nothing else could match"

Handkerchief, handkerchief — I'm so bored of that stupid hanky. Couldn't he have given his wife flowers like everyone else? No one even carries hankies anymore. Now, a green-eyed monster — that's definitely more exciting — nice one Shakey.

Act 4, Scene 1

Othello thinks he hears Cassio confessing to having a relationship with Desdemona so he plans to kill them both.

Othello seems to be completely under Iago's Power...

- Iago continues to **torture** Othello by talking about Desdemona and Cassio's alleged affair. Othello **has a seizure**.
- Iago **persuades** Othello to **eavesdrop** on a conversation between himself and **Cassio**. Iago asks Cassio about **Bianca** but Othello **thinks** they're talking about **Desdemona**.
- **Lodovico** delivers a letter **summoning** Othello back to **Venice** and appointing Cassio as his replacement as **governor** of Cyprus. Othello **mistakes** Desdemona's **happiness** as affection for **Cassio**, so he **hits** her.

Iago **never** leaves the **stage** in this scene and he is in **complete control**:

1) He continues to use **innuendo** and **suggestion** to manipulate Othello, asking questions like **"Have you not hurt your head?"** (line 59) to imply that Othello has grown the horns of a cuckold. He also exploits the **double meaning** of the word **"Lie"** (line 34) to force Othello to **draw his own conclusions** about Cassio and Desdemona's **relationship** (see p.14 for more on Iago's persuasive techniques).

> *A cuckold is a man with an unfaithful wife.*

2) Othello starts to **mimic** Iago's **language**. His exclamation **"Goats and monkeys!"** (line 265) echoes Iago's **taunts** in Act 3, Scene 3, lines 400-401 and shows how the **image** of Cassio and Desdemona as **animals ready to mate** has been **torturing** him.

3) Iago **manipulates situations** as well as characters — he **lowers his voice** to ask Cassio about Bianca, knowing that Othello's **"jealousy"** (line 101) will make him understand Cassio's comments **"Quite in the wrong"** (line 103).

> *The misunderstanding eavesdropper is traditionally a comedy routine — the eavesdropper realises his mistake just in time. Othello's misunderstanding is tragic because he only realises his mistake when it's already too late.*

Othello has Completely Changed

Othello's **transformation**, which took place in **Act 3, Scene 3**, is clear in this scene — Iago points out that **"He is much changed"** (line 270). Othello **loses control** of his actions and speech.

He loses his nobility and becomes more savage

Othello **physically loses control**, falling into **"an epilepsy"** (line 50) and **striking Desdemona**. His decision to **eavesdrop** on Cassio is a **cowardly** and **underhand** action which contrasts with his earlier **openness**: **"I must be found"** (1.2.30). **Lodovico** is shocked to see that **"the noble Moor"** (line 266) has succumbed to savage jealousy. He represents **Venetian civilisation** and he's **alarmed** by Othello's **barbarity**.

He loses his role as a leader and becomes a follower

Not only does Othello lose his **position** as **governor** in this scene, he also loses his air of **authority**. He asks Iago **questions** instead of **commanding** him: **"How shall I murder him, Iago?"** (line 169). Iago, in turn, starts **commanding** Othello: **"Do it not with poison; strangle her in her bed"** (line 206).

He acts less like a husband and more like a soldier

The **conflict** between Othello's two roles as a **husband** and a **soldier** is evident in this scene — previously he acted as **peacekeeper**, breaking up the **fight** between Cassio and Roderigo (2.3.163-172), before returning to **bed** with his **wife**. Now Othello is the one **creating violence** as he **reverts** to his role as a **soldier** — he becomes more **decisive** and his **language** becomes more **warlike** and **aggressive**. He threatens to **"chop [Desdemona] into messes!"** (line 199).

The Female characters are Treated Badly

This scene shows how the **men** in the play **abuse** the female characters:

1) Iago's **misogyny** continues as he suggests that **most women** are **adulteresses** — he says that there's **"many a beast then in a populous city"** (line 63) since **so many women** make their husbands **cuckolds**. He also describes Desdemona as **"wanton"** (line 71) and **"foul"** (line 200).

2) Cassio treats Bianca **cruelly**, mocking her affection for him, and describing her as **"the monkey"** (line 128) and **"the bauble"** (line 135). When Bianca enters, her **reaction** shows how **hurtful** Cassio's **behaviour** is.

3) Othello **hits** Desdemona, **humiliating** her in **public**. She has become so **submissive** that she can only **obey** his order to get **"Out of my sight!"** (line 247). Although Lodovico is **shocked**, he does **little** to **protect** her.

Act 4, Scene 2

Desdemona is confused and upset when Othello accuses her of having an affair.

Emilia **Defends** Desdemona's **Innocence**, but Othello **Isn't Convinced**...

- Othello asks Emilia about Desdemona and Cassio's supposed affair. She assures him that they're innocent.
- Othello interrogates Desdemona. She defends herself, but Othello thinks she's lying.
- Roderigo confronts Iago because his attempts to woo Desdemona have come to nothing.

See p.61 for more on religion.

This scene is full of **religious imagery**:

1) Both **Othello** and **Desdemona** associate themselves with **Christianity** in this scene. When Othello accuses Desdemona of being a "**strumpet**" (line 81), Desdemona **defends** herself, saying "**No, as I am a Christian**" (line 81). This highlights her **innocent nature** and links Desdemona with **Christ**, a connection which **continues** through to Act 5, Scene 2 when her **life** is a "**sacrifice**" (5.2.65) for what Othello sees as the **greater good**.

2) Othello refers to **Christianity** and **heaven** in an attempt to **regain** his sense of **honour** and **morality**. The fact that Othello refers to himself in the **third person** — "**that cunning whore of Venice / That married with Othello**" (lines 88-89) — could suggest that he feels he is **losing** his **identity**.

3) Othello's **language** makes Desdemona's perceived **betrayal** take on a **spiritual significance** — he calls her a "**rose-lipped cherubin**" (line 62) that has turned "**grim as hell**" (line 63). Othello believes that Desdemona's **angelic** appearance **increases** her sin as beneath it he believes she is "**false as hell**" (line 38).

Emilia takes on the **Opposite Role** to Iago

1) Emilia is the **only** character to realise that Othello has been manipulated by "**some eternal villain**" (line 129) and even suggests that the motive was "**to get some office**" (line 131), but she never suspects her **own husband**.

2) As Othello **quizzes** Emilia about Desdemona's fidelity, she replies with **definite** answers. Her repeated assertion that she has "**Never**" had any reason to doubt Desdemona (lines 6, 7 and 9) contrasts with Iago's **implied suggestions** which make other characters assume the **worst** (see p.14).

3) Unlike Iago, Emilia provides **real evidence** for Desdemona's fidelity and shows the **strength** of her **loyalty** to her mistress when she says she would "**Lay down [her] soul**" (bet her soul) that Desdemona is **honest** (line 12). By this point, however, Othello has **already** made up his mind that Desdemona is **unfaithful** — "**my heart is turned to stone**" (4.1.181-182).

Iago constantly **Changes** his **Role**

1) Despite advising Othello to "**strangle her in her bed**" in the previous scene (4.1.206), Iago now **acts sympathetically** towards Desdemona. He comforts her, "**weep not; all things shall be well**" (line 170), and **assures** her that Othello is **only** affected by the "**business of the state**" (line 165).

2) When **Roderigo** enters, Iago has to display **a different persona**. Roderigo comes close to discovering Iago's true nature, saying that Iago's "**words and performances are no kin together**" (lines 182-183). However, Iago easily **manipulates** him with lies and **flattery** to get him back on side: "**I see there's mettle in thee**" (line 204).

© Johan Persson / ArenaPAL

Practice Questions

Q1 Compare how Othello behaves in Act 4, Scene 1 with his actions in the first two acts of the play. Analyse how he has changed.

Q2 Using Act 4, Scene 2 as a starting point, analyse the importance of religious language and imagery throughout the play.

"Heaven truly knows that thou art false as hell"

If you're going to insult someone, you might as well sound intellectual while you're at it. Try using a line from 'Othello' — ask if they're "light of brain" or call them a "base notorious knave". You wouldn't want to cross Shakespeare — that "scurvy fellow"...

Act 4, Scene 3

After the male characters leave, Desdemona and Emilia are left alone on stage.

Emilia and Desdemona **Confide** in **Each Other...**

- Othello **orders** Desdemona to go to **bed** and tells her to **dismiss Emilia**.
- Desdemona tells Emilia the story of her mother's **maid**, Barbary, and sings her **'willow' song**.
- Desdemona and Emilia **discuss** their different views on **infidelity** and **marriage**.

The relationship between **Desdemona** and **Emilia** shown in this scene **contrasts** with the male relationships in *Othello*:

1) Male relationships in *Othello* are **hierarchical** — this is emphasised by the importance of **military ranks**. Although Emilia is Desdemona's **lady-in-waiting**, they talk **openly** about men and relationships as if they were **equals**.

2) However, at times their relationship **parallels** that of their **husbands** more closely. Like Iago's relationship with Othello, Emilia seems more **worldly** than Desdemona. Whereas Desdemona **can't believe** that there is "**any such woman**" (line 82) who would be **unfaithful** to her husband, Emilia is more **realistic**.

Different **Omens Foreshadow** Desdemona's **Death**

1) Desdemona asks Emilia to "**shroud**" her in her **wedding sheets** "**If I do die before thee**" (line 23). This suggests that Desdemona might be **anticipating** her own **death** because in **Elizabethan times** wives were sometimes **buried** in the sheets of their **wedding night**.

2) The **'willow' song** also foreshadows Desdemona's **death**. There are **parallels** between **Desdemona** and her mother's maid, Barbary, who sang the **'willow' song**:

> Barbary was "**in love**" but her lover "**proved mad**" (line 26) and "**did forsake her**" (line 27). Desdemona **loves** Othello, but he has been driven **mad** by jealousy. Barbary "**died singing it**" (line 29) and Desdemona says the song "**Will not go from my mind**" (line 30). This is a further indication that **death** is **on her mind**. Willow trees are traditionally **symbols** of **lost love**, hinting that Desdemona has already **metaphorically 'lost'** Othello.

The melancholy 'willow' song contrasts with Iago's drinking songs in Act 2, Scene 3.

3) Desdemona **mistakenly** sings "**Let nobody blame him; his scorn I approve**" (line 49) before correcting herself. This echoes her assertion that "**my love doth so approve him / That even his stubbornness, his checks, his frowns / ...have grace and favour**" (lines 18-20). She refuses to **blame** Othello because of her **love** for him. Her mistake also **anticipates** her refusal to blame Othello for her **death** — she blames "**Nobody — I myself**" (5.2.125).

Emilia's speech **Challenges Gender Inequality**

Emilia's speech about **marriage** and **adultery** has been used by **feminist critics** as evidence that, in *Othello*, Shakespeare was **challenging** the Elizabethan **patriarchy** (see p.38-9).

A patriarchy is a society where men hold all or most of the power, and women have little or none.

1) Emilia draws attention to the **double standard** between men and women: men have affairs for "**sport**" (line 96) and commit **adultery**, but expect their **wives** to remain **chaste**. She thinks that it's **unfair** to condemn women for the **same crime** and blames men if their wives "**fall**" (line 86) — "**it is their husbands' faults**" (line 85) and "**The ills we do, their ills instruct us so**" (line 102). The phrase "**Let husbands know**" (line 92) suggests that she's addressing the **audience**, and not just Desdemona.

2) She also seems to want **equality** with men in **marriage**, and **defends** her **gender** by saying that women "**have sense like them: they see and smell**" (line 93). She blames husbands "**If wives do fall**" (line 86) and argues that **wives** should be able to have "**revenge**" (line 92) if their husbands **cheat** or "**strike**" them (line 89). She makes the case for women to be treated like **people** and not as **objects** — in **contrast** with the way the **male** characters **objectify women** in *Othello*.

3) Although Emilia **strongly argues** her point about **equality** between men and women, both Desdemona and Emilia are **ultimately** concerned with **obeying** their **husbands**. Desdemona says "**We must not now displease him**" (line 16) and Emilia's **justification** of **adultery** revolves around the idea that it could **benefit** her husband: "**who would not make her husband a cuckold to make him a monarch?**" (lines 74-75).

4) By the **end** of the play, both Desdemona and Emilia, the two women who could be seen to **challenge** the **traditional patriarchy** (see p.60-61) have been **killed** and **silenced** by their **husbands**.

Act 5, Scene 1

Iago has convinced Roderigo to kill Cassio — they wait for him in the darkness outside Bianca's lodgings.

Roderigo and Iago **Attack Cassio** in the **Dark**...

- Roderigo **attacks Cassio**, but is **unsuccessful**. Cassio injures Roderigo, then Iago **stabs Cassio** in the leg and exits.
- **Othello** hears Cassio calling out in **pain** and thinks Iago has **killed him**. Othello leaves to **murder Desdemona**.
- Iago returns and **feigns ignorance** of what has happened. He then **stabs and kills Roderigo**.
- **Bianca** is **distraught** to see Cassio injured. Iago **accuses her** of being **involved** in the attack on Cassio.

This scene is **reminiscent** of the fight between Roderigo and Cassio in **Act 2, Scene 3**.

1) The darkness again causes **confusion**. Iago adopts the role of the **confused bystander** that Othello took in Act 2, Scene 3. Like Othello, Iago asks lots of **questions**: "**Who's there?**" (line 48) and "**Who is't that cried?**" (line 75).

> *Elizabethan plays were performed in the afternoon — the questions establish that this is a night scene.*

2) In Act 2, Scene 3, Othello **steps in** to stop the **fight** between Montano and Cassio, but in Act 5, Scene 1 he **stands back** to watch the **chaos**. He has **lost** his previous **nobility** — he's **actively involved** in the plot to **kill Cassio**.

Iago **Still** seems to be **In Control**...

1) This scene is the **last time** that any character looks to **Iago** for **guidance**.

- Roderigo is willing to **kill Cassio**, despite having "**no great devotion to the deed**" (line 8). Iago has given him "**satisfying reasons**" (line 9) after Roderigo's **accusations against** him in Act 4, Scene 2.
- Othello thinks that Iago has **killed Cassio** and says "**Thou teachest me**" (line 33). He declares that Desdemona's bed "**lust-stained, shall with lust's blood be spotted**" (line 36) which **echoes** Iago's earlier suggestion that he kill Desdemona in "**the bed she hath contaminated**" (4.1.207).

© Johan Persson / ArenaPAL

2) Iago continues to **improvise**, using the **situations** he's faced with to his **advantage**. He has a **practical** attitude to murder — he doesn't **care** who kills who between Cassio and Roderigo because **both deaths** will **benefit** him. He uses the **darkness** and **confusion** as an opportunity to attack **both** of them.

3) He also **accuses Bianca** of being involved in the **attack** on **Cassio** in order to **divert attention** away from **himself**. He uses **leading questions** that he already **knows** the answer to, in order to **convince** the other bystanders.

... but his plans are **Starting** to **Unravel**

1) Iago realises that he is in a **precarious** position, and that his **fortunes** are becoming **increasingly uncertain**. He tells Roderigo that the **attack** on Cassio "**makes us, or it mars us**" (line 4) and in the final lines of the scene, he tells the audience "**This is the night / That either makes me, or fordoes me quite**" (lines 128-129).

2) Iago's **failure** to orchestrate **Cassio's death** suggests that **his luck is running out**. Previously, he had been able to **control** situations **perfectly**, but now his **power** is **waning** — he **only** manages to **injure** Cassio, who is then able to **explain** his possession of the **handkerchief** in Act 5, Scene 2.

3) **Roderigo** is the **first character** to finally see Iago as he **really is**, calling him an "**inhuman dog**" (line 62). His **letters** are important in **confirming** Iago's **guilt** in Act 5, Scene 2. Bianca also seems to question Iago's **honesty** when she claims that she is "**as honest / As you that thus abuse me**" (lines 122-123).

Practice Questions

Q1 Using Act 4, Scene 3 as a starting point, assess the extent to which *Othello* challenges gender roles.

Q2 'By the end of Act 5, Scene 1, Iago's downfall is inevitable.' To what extent do you agree with this statement?

"This is the night / That either makes me or fordoes me quite"

So, tonight's the night. Either all of Iago's plans will succeed and everyone will kill everyone else, or he'll be found out and brutally tortured for the rest of his life *fingers crossed*... Oh. He gets found out AFTER everyone's already dead? How unfortunate...

Act 5, Scene 2

This scene is set in the very personal space of Othello and Desdemona's bedroom, but the events are very public.

Othello **Kills Desdemona** and then **Commits Suicide**...

- Othello tells Desdemona he's going to **kill her**. She **begs** for her life, but he **smothers her** on their bed.
- Emilia **discovers** the **murder** and tells Othello that Desdemona was **innocent**. **Montano, Gratiano** and **Iago** enter the bedroom when they hear Emilia's cries. When Emilia finds out that **Iago** used the **handkerchief** to prove Desdemona's **guilt**, she **confesses** that she **stole** it and **accuses Iago** of deceiving Othello.
- Iago **kills Emilia** and runs away. He's **caught** and brought back but he **refuses** to **explain** his **actions**.
- Othello **commits suicide**. Cassio is given responsibility for **torturing** Iago.

The **setting** of Othello and Desdemona's **bedroom** is significant:

1) **Earlier** in the play, the bedroom symbolised the **consummation** of Othello and Desdemona's **marriage** — Othello refers to "**the fruits**" (2.3.9) that are to come as he takes his wife to **bed** in Act 2, Scene 3. However, by Act 5, Scene 2 it has become a place of **death** and **despair**, just as Desdemona seemed to **anticipate** in Act 4, Scene 3 (see p.20).

2) This scene **emphasises** that Desdemona and Othello's **entire relationship** has played out in **public**. Initially, they are **alone** in their private marital bedroom, but by the **end** of the scene, the room is full of **officials**.

3) The **staging** of this scene in **one room** containing so **many characters** makes it seem **claustrophobic** and it **intensifies** the drama. On stage, the bed would probably have been surrounded by **curtains** which could be partly drawn to **focus** the **attention** of the audience even more **closely** on the events taking place on the **bed**.

Othello tries to **Justify** his **Actions**

> Othello associates himself with God by calling his sorrow "heavenly" (line 21) — it's written in the Bible that God disciplines those he loves (Hebrews 12:6). Othello thinks that he's punishing Desdemona for her own good.

Othello seems **confused** as he tries to explain his motives — it's as if he's **unclear why** he has to kill Desdemona.

1) He **initially** claims, "**It is the cause**" (line 1) — he must kill Desdemona for the 'crime' of **adultery** that he believes she has committed. He wants to **justify** the murder to himself and **deny** that he is motivated by a loss of **honour**.

2) However, his **language** indicates that **honour** is actually at the forefront of his mind — he later claims that he is an "**honourable murderer**" (line 291) and seems to think that in killing Desdemona, he can **restore** some **honour** — "**she must die, else she'll betray more men**" (line 6). He sees Desdemona's death as "**a sacrifice**" (line 65) and thinks that if she is **dead** she cannot bring his, or her own, **honour** into any more **disrepute**.

3) Othello hopes to **restore** Desdemona to her **former glory** — if she is **dead**, she can no longer **sin** and he can remember the **idealised woman** he believed she was before. **Paradoxically**, he thinks that **killing Desdemona** is the **only** way to ensure that their **love survives**. He tells her sleeping form "**I will kill thee / And love thee after**" (lines 18-19).

4) Othello sees himself as an **agent** of **justice**. He's **tempted** to let Desdemona live — her breath "**dost almost persuade / Justice to break her sword!**" (lines 16-17), but feels that he has "**just grounds**" (line 139) and **justice** forces him to act.

5) Othello seems to think that Desdemona is **fated** to **die**, and he cannot **prevent** it. He describes her as an "**ill-starred wench**" (line 270) and compares her skin to "**monumental alabaster**" (line 5) which brings to mind stone statues of the **dead** lying on top of their **tombs** — he sees Desdemona as **already dead**.

The **Tragedy** of Desdemona's **Death** is **Heightened**

1) At the **beginning** of the scene, Othello and Desdemona's **lines** run into each other. This is a **distorted version** of Act 2, Scene 1, where the **harmony** of Desdemona and Othello's **marriage** was obvious as they **finished** each other's **lines**. In Act 5, Scene 2, each character says only a **few words** before the **other** starts speaking. Even **before** Othello kills Desdemona, it's **clear** that Iago has **destroyed** the beauty and love of their relationship.

2) In spite of everything Othello has done to her, Desdemona still **defends** him. When Emilia asks Desdemona who's to blame for her death, she replies, "**I myself**" (line 125) and asks her to, "**Commend me to my kind lord**" (line 126). This **highlights** the **strength** of the love which Iago **destroyed**.

3) Desdemona seems to offer **forgiveness** to Othello and **blames herself**, whilst maintaining that she's "**guiltless**" (line 123). Some critics have seen Desdemona as a **Christlike figure** — she succumbs to a **guiltless death** as a result of another's **sins** (Othello's **jealousy**), she doesn't seem to physically **resist** her tragic fate, and **forgives** her killer.

4) Othello doesn't **want** to kill Desdemona, but feels **compelled** to. The play's tragedy is emphasised when he discovers that he **murdered** his wife without **cause** — he **still loves her** and no longer **believes** that she had to die.

Act 5, Scene 2

Emilia seems to **Redeem Herself**

1) In spite of the **danger**, Emilia bravely **stands up** for Desdemona's **honesty** and claims **"I care not for thy sword"** (line 164). She ensures that both Iago and Othello are **punished**, and acts as a **reminder** of Desdemona's **chastity** and the **love** that she and Othello once shared.

2) She seems to be innocently **unaware** of Iago's **maliciousness** — this is shown by the fact that she **repeats "My husband!" three times** (lines 141, 145 and 148) in shock. When his **deception** becomes clear, she is **quick** to condemn him — **"may his pernicious soul / Rot half a grain a day"** (lines 154-155).

3) Emilia seems to **believe** that her **final** actions have **redeemed** her **betrayal** of Desdemona — she **reveals Iago's deception, confesses** to stealing the **handkerchief**, and makes sure **justice is served**. She thinks that she is **destined** to go to heaven: **"So come my soul to bliss, as I speak true"** (line 248).

Religion seems to **Preoccupy** everyone

Iago's refusal to explain his motives could suggest that he's a motiveless force for evil — a Satan-like Vice character (see p.26).

1) This scene is full of **religious imagery** as the **fate** of each character's **soul** becomes a focus:

   - Othello continues to **associate** himself with **Christianity**, even **connecting** himself with the **vengeful Christian God** (see p.22). He asks Desdemona if she has **"prayed"** (line 25) as he doesn't want to **damn her soul**.
   - Emilia **defends** her mistress by describing **Desdemona** as an **"angel"** (line 131) who is **"heavenly true"** (line 136) but calling **Othello** a **"devil"** (lines 132 and 134). She hopes to **redeem herself** in the play's **final scene**.
   - Othello accuses Iago of being a **"demi-devil"** (line 298), and says **"If that thou be'st a devil, I cannot kill thee"** (line 284). He **wounds** Iago, but Iago doesn't **die**, leaving the **audience** to draw their **own conclusions**.

2) In the **Folio** edition of the play the **"base Indian"** (line 343) that Othello **compares** himself to is printed **"base Iudean"** (or **Judean**). **"Judean"** could refer to the Biblical **betrayal** of Jesus by **Judas Iscariot** and **furthers** the analogy between **Desdemona** and **Christ** (see p.22).

Othello tries to **Regain** his **Nobility**

Othello's **final speech** could either suggest that he has regained his **nobility** or that he has remained **self-centred** (see p.59).

1) Othello **distances himself** from the murder he's committed by describing Desdemona in an **abstract** sense: she is **"the light"** (line 7), a **"rose"** (line 13) and a **"pearl"** (line 343). He also speaks about himself in the third person: **"one, not easily jealous"** (line 341) and seems unwilling to accept the blame for his actions, asking **"Who can control his fate?"** (line 263).

2) His final speech could suggest that Othello is **self-centred** because he seems focused on **himself** rather than on **Desdemona's murder**. He's **preoccupied** with the **"service"** (line 335) he has done the **state**, and **mending** his **reputation**.

3) His suicide could also be seen as a **cowardly escape** from the **punishment** that he faced, or as a **return** to nobility. Othello sees it as an act of **redemption** (see p.25), **atoning** for Desdemona's murder by **ending** his **own** life. However, this **conflicts** with the **traditional Christian** view that suicide is a **sin** and could suggest that he has **returned** to the Elizabethan stereotype of a **pagan** and **savage** past.

© Marilyn Kingwill / ArenaPAL

Practice Questions

Q1 Using Act 5, Scene 2 as a starting point, do you think that Iago's plots are successful?

Q2 'Othello regains his former nobility in his speech and actions at the end of the play.' How far do you agree with this statement? Use evidence from the text to support your answer.

"No way but this, / Killing myself, to die upon a kiss"

Well, after all that murder and suicide I'm feeling a little depressed. Turns out that 'The Tragedy of Othello, the Moor of Venice' was pretty tragic after all. It just goes to show — you really can judge a book by its cover. If that cover says 'Tragedy' on it, anyway...

Othello

Othello isn't just an age-old board game, it's also the name of this play, and coincidentally its protagonist.
He's an ambiguous character who's noble and civilised at the beginning of the play, and savage and violent by the end.

Othello is a **Character** of **Contradictions**

1) Othello's **character** is full of **oppositions**:

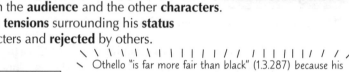

- Othello is a **black man**, but is **accepted** by many of the **white Venetians**.
- He was a **slave**, but is now a **general in the Venetian army** — as a **mercenary** (**hired soldier**) he still **serves** the Duke but he also has a **high rank**.
- He's a **fierce warrior** and a **loving husband**, so there's **conflict** between his **personal life** and **military role**.
- He's **modest**, and **admits** to his **insecurities** but is also **aware** of his **strengths**.
- **Initially**, he's **self-controlled** but by the **end** of the play he's **irrational** and **violent**.

2) Othello can be **viewed** in a **number of ways** by both the **audience** and the other **characters**. The **oppositions** in his **character** mean that there are **tensions** surrounding his **status** in **Venetian society** — he's **accepted** by some characters and **rejected** by others.

He's **Part** of **Society**, but is still an **Outsider**

> Othello "is far more fair than black" (1.3.287) because his ambiguity challenges the racial stereotype that blackness was associated with immorality. However, this line also reinforces the idea that whiteness or fairness equates with goodness.

Othello's both **inside** and **outside** Venetian society:

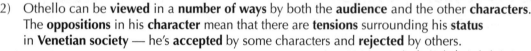

PART OF SOCIETY

1) He's **considered** an **important member** of society because of his **skill** as a **soldier** — the senate **"sent about three several quests"** to look for Othello (1.2.46). He's **trusted** to be in **full control** of the **army** and **Cyprus** and has been a **loyal servant**: **"I have done the state some service and they know't"** (5.2.335).
2) Othello is **accepted** by the **Venetians**, and he's **welcomed** into their **social circles**. Othello says that Brabantio **"loved me, oft invited me, / Still questioned me the story of my life"** (1.3.127-128). Even the **Duke** acknowledges Othello's **attractiveness**: **"I think this tale would win my daughter too"** (1.3.170).
3) Othello **involves** himself further with Venetian **society** by **marrying Desdemona**. Although Brabantio **rejects** their **love**, the Duke **accepts** the marriage, which shows that he sees Othello as **part** of **Venetian society**.

AN OUTSIDER

1) Othello is a **black man** in a **white society** — even though he adopts the **Venetian culture** and **religion** everyone **recognises** that he's **foreign** and **exotic**, and it's his **tale** of being an **outsider** that **wins** Desdemona.
2) Othello is often described using **racial language** — Roderigo and Iago call him **"the Moor"**, **"the thick-lips"** and **"an old black ram"** in the **first scene** alone (1.1.58, 1.1.67, 1.1.89). **Before** Othello **appears**, Brabantio, Roderigo and Iago have all **condemned him** — they **see** him as an **outsider** from the **start**.
3) At times, Othello **reinforces the idea** of being an **outsider**, either because he **recognises his exotic appeal** or because he's **self-conscious** of his **differences**. For example, he says **"Haply, for I am black / And have not those soft parts of conversation / That chamberers have"** which presents him as an outsider (3.3.260-262).

Iago uses Othello's **status** as an **outsider** to **play on** his **insecurities** — it helps **convince him** of Desdemona's **affair**.

His **Relationship** with **Desdemona** is **Problematic**

1) Most Venetian characters have **preconceptions** about **interracial marriage** — it's seen as being **"Against all rules of nature"** (1.3.101) and being **motivated purely** by the **sexual desires** of **"a lascivious Moor"** (1.1.127).
2) Despite the **scandal** of **marrying outside** their **race**, Othello and Desdemona **initially appear** to be **happy** and **in love**. Their **courtship** was **mutual** and their **meeting in Cyprus** in Act 2, Scene 1 reveals the **intensity** of their **relationship**. Othello seems **overcome** with **happiness**: **"I cannot speak... / ... it is too much of joy"** (2.1.190-191).
3) Othello's **struggle** to be both a **husband** and a **soldier** causes **tensions** — he **refuses** to be **distracted** from his **military duties**, and acknowledges that **"'tis the soldier's life / To have their balmy slumbers waked with strife"** (2.3.250-251).
4) Their relationship starts to **unravel** as Iago **exploits** Othello's **insecurities** about their **marriage** and the fact that he **doesn't** actually **know** his new wife **very well**. Iago **encourages** Othello to **admit** that their relationship is **"nature, erring from itself"** (3.3.225) and **reminds** him that Desdemona **"did deceive her father, marrying you"** (3.3.204).

Othello

Othello's Downfall is the Focus of the Play

1) Over the course of the play, **Othello** changes from being a **noble man** to being **plagued** with **"savage madness"** (4.1.55). His **transformation** is **sudden**, and is **driven** by jealousy — the **turning point** occurs in **Act 3, Scene 3**.

2) After Othello **gives in** to **jealousy**, the **effects** are **clear**. He **loses control** emotionally and **physically**, and becomes **violent**, striking Desdemona in **Act 4, Scene 1**. He loses his **eloquence**, and his **language** becomes **increasingly crude** and **incoherent**, as he shouts phrases like **"Fire and brimstone!"** (4.1.232).

3) Some critics have blamed Othello's **downfall** on his **own flaws** while others have blamed **Iago's influence**:

- **A.C. Bradley** blames Othello's **downfall** on **Iago** and argues that Othello is a **noble hero**. Bradley argues that Othello has a **trusting nature**, but does not give in **easily** to **jealousy**. Othello's **mind** is **poisoned** by **Iago**, who critics such as **Coleridge** see as an **evil being**. Iago **takes advantage** of Othello's **trust**, and **relentlessly drives** him towards **jealousy**.

- **F.R. Leavis** argues that Othello was **responsible** for his **downfall**, and that Iago **targeted** an **existing weakness** — that he's **predisposed to being jealous**. Leavis also thought that Othello becomes **preoccupied** with his **own emotions** and has a **tendency** to be **self-centred**. It could also be argued that Othello's **pride** is **responsible**, as he's **too concerned** with how Desdemona's **actions affect** his own **reputation**.

4) Other reasons for Othello's downfall could be that he **believes** that **all women** are **naturally promiscuous** and that it's **"fated"** for **men** to be **cuckolded** (3.3.273) — this means that he's **more likely** to **accept** that Desdemona is **unfaithful**.

5) It could also be **argued** that **society's treatment** of Othello **shaped** him — it could be that he starts to **believe** the **racist attacks** of the **other characters** and **behaves** the way they **expect** a **black man** to **behave**.

Othello Struggles to be Both a Soldier and a Lover

1) Initially, Othello **denies** that his **new marriage** will **distract** him from **military matters**. Othello says that he will not **"your serious and great business scant / For she is with me"** (1.3.264-265). Othello's **military reputation** is **integral** to his **identity** and his **status** in **Venetian society**, so he's very **proud** of it, and is **wary** of **losing it**.

2) However, his **personal life** and **professional life** are **incompatible** — his military career **suffers** as a result of **problems** in his **marriage**: **"Is this the noble Moor whom our full senate / Call all in all sufficient?"** (4.1.266-267).

3) Othello's **reputation** is **tied closely** to his **military career** as well as his **wife's fidelity**, and the two become **inseparable** to him — he links Desdemona to his **success** as a **soldier**. She even **replaces** his **career** as the **source** of his **pride** when he says **"Othello's occupation's gone"** (3.3.354) after he thinks she's been **unfaithful**.

4) Othello's **murder** of Desdemona could be seen as an **attempt** to **reassert** his **military identity** — he talks about the importance of **"honour"** (5.2.292) and sees her as a **"sacrifice"** (5.2.65).

5) Othello's **suicide** finally **ends** this **conflict** as the **soldier** within him **kills** the **"wrought"** and **passionate lover** (5.2.341) whose **love** led to **jealousy**. His **suicide** can also be seen as:

- An **act** of **redemption** — by taking his life he punishes himself for his **crime** and **regains** his **nobility**.

- An **attempt** to **salvage his reputation** — he could be **trying to prove** that he's a **better man** than **Iago** and isn't just a **common murderer**. His **death** also means he **avoids experiencing** the **inevitable loss** of his **reputation**.

- An **inevitability** — as a **tragic hero**, he has **no choice** but to **die**: **"No way but this"** (5.2.354). *For more on Aristotle's tragic theory see p.46.*

Practice Questions

Q1 Some critics argue that Othello and Iago can be seen as the two faces of good and evil. Other critics argue that they're two sides of the same man, illustrating different responses to jealousy. Which argument do you find more compelling?

Q2 'Othello is a noble and innocent victim, twisted out of all recognition by Iago's evil schemes'. To what extent do you agree with this statement? Give examples from the text in your answer.

"If virtue no delighted beauty lack, / Your son-in-law is far more fair than black"

'Oh, hello, Othello'. I wonder how many times people said that to him before he grew really sick of it... I reckon twice. Anyway, Othello's ambiguity can be a bit tricky, but this does mean you can use textual evidence to back up almost anything.

Iago

Iago's a sarcastic, cracker-hating parrot with his heart set on world domination... not really — he's actually far worse.
He's a complex and manipulative villain, hell bent on causing pain and suffering. The parrot looks quite fluffy in comparison...

He's the play's **Antagonist**

> An antagonist is a character who provides opposition to the protagonist (in this case Othello).

1) Iago is an **"ancient"** or **ensign** (1.1.33) — this was a **junior army officer** whose **main duty** was to be the **standard bearer**.

> A standard bearer carries an army's flag into battle.

2) Iago is **cold, cynical** and **disillusioned** — he **hates** the **world** and the **people** around him. He seems to take **pleasure** in **evil** and **disorder**, and never shows **remorse** for his **actions**. He doesn't seem to have a **clear motivation** for his **cruelty**.

3) He's a **clever schemer**, and he's **good** at **manipulating people**. He's **trusted** by **everyone** and **creates** the **illusion** that he's **"honest Iago"** (1.3.291) so it's **easy** for him to **influence** the other **characters** into **doing what he wants** them to.

4) It's difficult to know what Iago is **really like** because he's able to **adapt** to **every situation** or **character**. His **true nature** always stays **hidden**, and he even **lies** in his **soliloquies** which means that the **audience** can never **fully trust** what he says.

© Everett Collection / Rex Features

His **Motivations** are **Ambiguous**

> Iago could be named after the Spanish Saint Iago who was known as the 'Moor Killer' — this could suggest that Iago was racially motivated to destroy Othello.

1) Unlike other **Shakespearean villains**, who have **clear motives** for their **actions**, such as Claudius in *Hamlet*, Iago's **motives** are **never confirmed**, although he suggests **several**:

- He was **overlooked** for **promotion** — Iago thinks Cassio doesn't **deserve** to be **lieutenant** and he's **angry** with Othello for choosing Cassio who has **"never set a squadron in the field"** (1.1.22).
- He's **jealous** of Cassio's **"daily beauty"** which makes him feel **"ugly"** (5.1.19-20) — Cassio heightens Iago's insecurities, and Iago also **suspects** him of having **slept** with **Emilia**: **"I fear Cassio with my night-cap"** (2.1.298).
- Iago **suspects Othello** had an **affair** with **Emilia** — **"'twixt my sheets / He's done my office"** (1.3.381-382). He claims that he wants to **take revenge** on Othello by having an **affair** with **Desdemona**.
- He **lusts** after **Desdemona**, claiming **"Now I do love her too"** (2.1.282).
- He's **materialistic** — his **exploitation** of Roderigo is motivated by **greed** and **self-interest**: **"Thus do I ever make my fool my purse"** (1.3.377). Once Roderigo is **no more use** to Iago, he **kills** him.
- He's **generally racist** and **misogynistic** — he seems to **hate anyone** who's **different from himself**.

2) Iago is **inconsistent** about his **various motivations** so it's difficult to **believe** any of them — they seem more like **excuses** than **genuine motivations**. It could be said that Iago **loses sight** of his **own intentions**.

3) His **appetite** for **destruction** suggests that he has an **addiction** to **power, evil** or **control**. He **initially** just wants to throw **"chances of vexation"** (1.1.73) on Othello's **joy** — a **far cry** from the **devastation** he **ultimately causes**.

Some **Critics Argue** that Iago has **No Motivation**

1) At the end of the play Iago **refuses** to **explain his motives**: **"From this time forth I never will speak a word"** (5.2.301). This suggests that either he **doesn't have any** motives, or that he **won't reveal** them — this makes him seem even more **ruthless** and means that he **remains in control**.

2) Iago's **cruelty** is so **extreme** that some critics argue that there is **no reasonable motivation** to **justify** his **actions**. Critics such as **Samuel Coleridge** argue that Iago has **no real motives** and is **pure evil**. Coleridge calls Iago's **behaviour** "motiveless malignity" (see p.57).

3) Iago can also be seen as a kind of **'Vice' character**. 'Vice' characters **personified** **evil** and **immorality** in **medieval morality plays**. Although Iago is **more complex** than this, it's **likely** that Shakespeare was **influenced** by this **literary tradition**.

> Richard III is another Shakespearean character who's considered to be a 'Vice' figure.

4) Other critics consider Iago to be **simply** a **force of evil** who takes **enjoyment** from **causing pain**. He **tells Roderigo "If thou canst cuckold him, thou dost thyself a pleasure, me a sport"** (1.3.363-364).

Iago

Iago is a *Skilled Manipulator*

It could be argued that Iago's ultimate failure indicates that he's foolish to think that he can deceive everyone.

1) The **main characters trust** Iago, so he knows their minds **extremely well**. He gains their **confidence** by maintaining the illusion of having "**love and honesty**" (3.3.117), then **uses** what he **learns** against them. He can **manipulate them** so **effectively** because he knows their **weaknesses**.

2) Iago's **skills of manipulation** makes him a **director**, able to **control** the **other characters' actions**. For example, in **Act 4, Scene 1** he not only **tells Othello** to eavesdrop on him and Cassio, but he also tells him how to **interpret** it: "**mark the fleers, the gibes, and notable scorns / That dwell in every region of his face**" (4.1.82-83).

3) Iago is **constantly thinking** on his feet and uses **clever improvisation** to **take advantage** of **unexpected situations**. For example, in **Act 5, Scene 1**, he seizes an **opportunity** to **stab Roderigo** and **blame Bianca** for the fight.

4) Iago's **success** is also a **result** of his **versatility** — he **adapts** his **language** to **suit** the person he's **speaking to**. With **Desdemona** he appears to be a **trustworthy confidante**: "**Do not weep, do not weep: alas the day!**" (4.2.123). With **Roderigo**, he uses **commands** to **confidently direct** the **action**, and with **Othello** he uses **vulgar language** to **create** a **detailed image** of Desdemona and Cassio's **affair** to **torture** him (see p.49 for more on Iago's language).

5) Despite Iago's **cruelty**, he **appeals** both to the **audience** and the other **characters** because he has a **sense of humour**. He shares **knowing jokes** with the **audience**, calling himself "**honest**" and **denying** that he's playing "**the villain**" (2.3.326-327), and **entertains** the other characters with **bawdy stories**.

He has *Complicated Relationships* with *Men* and *Women*

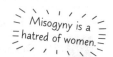
Misogyny is a hatred of women.

1) Iago doesn't have a **high opinion** of **women** and he has often been labelled a **misogynist**:

- Iago seems to **display** a **contempt** for **women** throughout the play. He suggests that women are **promiscuous** — claiming that they "**rise to play and go to bed to work**" (2.1.114) or **adulterous**: "**they do let heaven see the pranks / They dare not show their husbands**" (3.3.200-201).

- Iago's **marriage** to Emilia is **loveless** — she's **desperate** to **please him**, but he's **only interested** in **using her** to his **advantage**. When she steals the handkerchief, Iago just **snatches it** and calls her a "**foolish wife**" (3.3.301).

- Iago's **murder** of Emilia has been seen by **feminist critics** both as an **act** of **self-preservation** on Iago's part, and as an **attempt** to **silence a woman** who has **stood up** to her **husband**. Emilia says she's "**bound to speak**" (5.2.183) to **expose her husband's lies** despite Iago repeatedly trying to stop her: "**charm your tongue**" (5.2.181).

2) His relationships with **men** are even **more complicated** — Iago is **unable** to **connect** with people in an **ordinary way**:

- He hasn't got **any real friends** — he's probably **most open** with **Roderigo**, but Iago **uses** him for his **own gain**.

- His **relationship** with **Othello** is **complex** because Iago seems to **both love** and **hate** him.

- Despite Iago's hidden **hatred**, they have a **close relationship** which **grows more intense** as the **plot progresses**. Some critics **argue** that there are **homosexual undertones** in their **relationship** — **Laurence Olivier emphasised** this **aspect** by **kissing Othello** on the **lips** at the end of Act 3, Scene 3 when he played Iago in a **1938 production**.

- Evidence for **homosexual feelings** can also be seen in the **pleasure** that Iago takes in **ruining** Othello's **marriage**, as well as his **declarations of love**. At the end of **Act 3, Scene 3**, Othello's **conversation** with Iago has been said to **echo** an **Elizabethan wedding ceremony**: Iago says "**I am your own forever**" (3.3.476).

Practice Questions

Q1 A.C. Bradley argued that "evil is compatible, and even appears to ally itself easily, with exceptional powers of will and intellect." Do you think that this argument is backed up by Iago's character? Refer to the text in your answer.

Q2 Explain which motive you think is the most convincing justification for Iago's behaviour. Do you think that Iago's actions can reasonably be explained by his stated motives, or is he simply a motiveless force for evil?

"And what's he then that says I play the villain?"

*In answer to your question Iago, 'He's pretty much on the money'. Yes, Iago is very much the villain and yet strangely he's also one of the more attractive characters. Ah, the temptations of evil — reminds me of a time **before** I used my revision powers for good...*

Desdemona

Desdemona is an ambiguous character who's full of contradictions. This could be because her true character is distorted by the men in the play, so it's never clear who she truly is — she could be a single female lawyer for all I know...

Desdemona is a **Loving Daughter** and **Wife**

© Moviestore Collection Ltd

1) Desdemona is Brabantio's **beautiful young daughter**. She goes against her **father's wishes** by **marrying Othello**, a **black man**, rather than one of her **Venetian suitors**.

2) Desdemona sees that her marriage has given her a **"divided duty"** (1.3.179) but stands by her **decision** to marry Othello. Even though she **acknowledges** a **duty** to her father she's **strong-willed** and **authoritative**: **"So much I challenge that I may profess"** (1.3.186).

3) She **promises** to be as **faithful** to Othello as **her mother** was to **Brabantio**: **"so much duty as my mother showed / To you, preferring you before her father"** (1.3.184-185). Brabantio **disowns her**, saying **"I am glad at soul I have no other child"** (1.3.194).

4) Despite **Brabantio's warning** that **"She has deceived her father and may thee"** (1.3.290) she's an **obedient, loving** and **loyal wife**. She **can't believe** Othello would be drawn into **jealousy** because she never gives him **"cause"** (3.4.156) and she **defends** him to her **death**.

She's both **Strong-willed** and **Obedient**

Desdemona is a **complex character** — at times she appears **independent**, but at others she appears **submissive**:

ASSERTIVE

1) Desdemona is a **white, upper-class** Venetian and would have been **expected** to **marry someone** of the same **class** and **race**, but she **rejects society's expectations** and marries **Othello** instead. This **contradicts** Brabantio's **view** of her as **"A maiden never bold / Of spirit, so still and quiet"** (1.3.94-95).

2) Desdemona **"was half the wooer"** in her **relationship** with **Othello** (1.3.174). She leaves behind her **familiar world** of Venice to go with Othello to Cyprus. She refuses to be **"A moth of peace"** (1.3.253) and firmly argues that she **"did love the Moor to live with him"** (1.3.245).

3) She's **described** in **military terms** as a **"fair warrior"** (2.1.176) which shows her **strength of character**.

4) She's **assertive** in her **marriage** when she takes up **Cassio's cause** and tries to **persuade Othello** of his **lieutenant's virtues**: **"I'll intermingle every thing he does / With Cassio's suit"** (3.3.25-26).

SUBMISSIVE

1) In the **second half** of the play Desdemona becomes **increasingly vulnerable** to Othello's **anger**. He **hits her** in **public** and calls her a **"strumpet"** (4.2.80) and a **"whore"** (4.2.85).

2) Despite this, she **defends Othello** when she says **"we must think men are not gods"** (3.4.144). She seems to **blame herself** for his **anger** and **accepts** his **abuse** — even when he **strikes** her, Desdemona **acknowledges his authority** and continues to be obedient: **"We must not now displease him"** (4.3.14-16).

3) Even after Othello's **verbal threats** and **physical abuse** Desdemona **continues to be obedient** and **loyal**. She tells Othello that she's **"Your wife, my lord; your true and loyal wife"** (4.2.33).

4) The way that she's **smothered** to **death** emphasises that she's become **passive** and **defenceless** (see p.29).

Iago **successfully persuades** Othello that Desdemona's **unfaithful** partly because she's **so independent**. It's **ironic** that her **decision** to **betray her father** to **marry Othello** becomes **one** of the **reasons** that Othello starts to **distrust her**.

She **Appears** to be quite **Naive**

1) In **Elizabethan society** marrying **outside your race** would have been **unusual** and **scandalous** and Desdemona also marries Othello **without knowing him** particularly well. It could be argued that Brabantio was **right** to be **cautious** about Desdemona's **decision**.

2) Although she's **confident** about the marriage at first, Desdemona soon reveals her **naivety** about **marriage** — she **refuses** to **believe** that **unfaithful wives exist**: **"I do not think there is any such woman"** (4.3.82). Because the idea of **infidelity** is **unthinkable** to her, she **doesn't realise** that Othello **suspects her** — this emphasises her **innocence**.

3) She **doesn't understand** Othello's **anger**, and is **confused** by his **accusations**. When he accuses her of **infidelity** she says **"I understand a fury in your words / But not the words"** (4.2.31-32). Her **bewilderment** makes her seem **childlike** — she **admits "I am a child to chiding"** (4.2.113).

Desdemona

Desdemona was *Chaste* and *Virtuous*

1) The fact that Desdemona is **faithful** and a good "**Christian**" (4.2.81) **heightens** the **tragedy** of her **death**. Her **innocence** is **emphasised** by her **frequent association** with **light** and **heaven**: "**the divine Desdemona**" (2.1.73).

2) Some **critics** believe that Desdemona is a **contradiction** — she **appears** to be **chaste** but she shows an **awareness** of **sexuality**. For example, she has a **bawdy conversation** with Iago in **Act 2, Scene 1**. However, Desdemona is a **young bride** who would be **anticipating** the **consummation** of her **marriage** — she would have been expected to have some **sexual desires**.

> - **Harold Bloom** argues that Desdemona **died** without ever **consummating her marriage**. If they had consummated it, Othello would have **realised** that she was a **virgin** and hadn't **cheated** on him with Cassio.
> - Other critics argue that Othello and Desdemona **did consummate** their marriage and Iago persuades Othello to **believe** in the **racist idea** that he **polluted Desdemona's purity** by consummating their marriage, because he was **black**: "**Her name that was as fresh / ...is now begrimed and black / As mine own face**" (3.3.383-385).

3) The **symbolism** of Desdemona's **murder** is **ironic** as she's **smothered** while in her **wedding sheets** — the sheets that would have been **associated** with **love** and **consummation** are now **linked** to **death** and the **end** of their **marriage**.

She's one of the *Main Victims* in the *Play*

The name Desdemona means 'the unfortunate' in Greek.

1) Desdemona is **treated unfairly** by **several men** in the play:

> - **Brabantio** — **disowns** her for **marrying Othello**.
> - **Roderigo** — wants to **commit adultery** with her.
> - **Iago** — **uses her** goodness for his **own revenge**.
> - **Othello** — **assumes** she's **guilty** and **murders** her.

2) Desdemona seems to **accept** her "**wretched fortune**" (4.2.127). In **Act 4, Scene 3** she seems to **anticipate** her death — she sings a **song** which **mirrors her life** and is **haunted** by the thought: "**That song tonight / Will not go from my mind**" (4.3.29-30). This creates **dramatic irony** for the **audience** who know Othello's plan.

3) She **maintains** her **innocence** throughout the **final scene** — the only **sins** she has **committed** "**are loves I bear to [Othello]**" (5.2.40). She **emphasises** her own **innocence repeatedly**: "**I never did / Offend you in my life**" (5.2.58-59) and "**A guiltless death I die**" (5.2.123). Emilia calls her an "**angel**", "**heavenly true**" and that she was "**too fond of her most filthy bargain**" (5.2.131, 136 and 156), **creating pathos** about her **death**.

4) Desdemona's **final words** are **ambiguous** and can be **interpreted** in **different ways**:

> **EMILIA:** O, who hath done this deed?
> **DESDEMONA:** Nobody — I myself — farewell. (5.2.124-125).

They could suggest:
- that she's **taken ownership** of her **own death** and she **blames herself** for Othello's **behaviour**.
- that she's still a **loyal wife** — even in **death**, she tries to **protect** and **defend Othello**.
- that she **forgives** Othello for his **treatment** of her and **still loves** him.

There's even **more tragedy** at the end as Othello **realises** her **innocence** — he **recognises** that she is a "**heavenly sight**" (5.2.276) and **grieves** for the wife who he has **killed**: "**O Desdemon! Dead, Desdemon. Dead!**" (5.2.279).

Practice Questions

Q1 Desdemona seems to defend Othello's abuse by saying "Let nobody blame him, his scorn I approve" (4.3.49). Do you think that Desdemona accepts or challenges the patriarchal society? Write a case for both sides of the argument.

Q2 'Desdemona's naivety meant that her marriage was always going to end unhappily, even without Iago's interfering'. To what extent do you agree with this statement? Give examples from the text in your answer.

"Thou art rash as fire, to say / That she was false: O, she was heavenly true!"

And thus poor Desdemona became Deademona. Perhaps that joke was a little off colour — much like Desdemona's rotting corpse... Okay, that really was too much. I'm having a pretty Gothic day I'm afraid, and I've got death on the brain.

Cassio

You'd think with a name like Cassio, he'd be most comfortable working as a watch-man... but in fact he's a lieutenant. Iago reckons Cassio's not much of a soldier, and he's probably right — maybe Cassio should reconsider his position.

Cassio is **Othello's Second** in **Command**

Florence had a strong cultural reputation at the time, so Florentines were generally seen to have a respectable standing in society (see p.54).

1) **Michael Cassio** is Othello's **lieutenant** in the **Venetian army**. He is a **Florentine**, which makes him an **outsider** in **Venetian** society, like **Othello**. He's very **loyal** to **Othello** and **helped** him to **court Desdemona** at the **beginning** of their relationship.

2) He can be **easily led** and **trusting**, which is why he's an **easy victim** for **Iago's schemes**. He's **charming** and **attractive**, which makes Iago **jealous** of his "**daily beauty**" (5.1.19).

3) He appears **chivalrous** and **honest** — he's described as "**Good Michael**" (2.3.1) and "**a proper man**" (1.3.386). He's clearly **proud** of his "**breeding**" and **good manners** (2.1.98). His **reputation** is **important** to him and he's concerned with **maintaining appearances**.

4) **Despite** his gentlemanly **manner**, Cassio doesn't **treat everyone** with the **same respect** — his **behaviour** towards his **lover**, Bianca, is **cruel** and **thoughtless**.

He seems to be an **Intellectual**

1) Iago **portrays** Cassio as a "**great arithmetician**" and a "**bookish theoric**" (1.1.19 and 24). Iago tries to present Cassio's **intelligence** as a **negative characteristic**, by suggesting that Cassio is **all theory** and **no practice**. Iago compares him to a "**spinster**" to **feminise him** because he knows so little about war (1.1.24).

2) Iago's **criticism** that "**Mere prattle without practice / Is all his soldiership**" (1.1.26-27) is **proven accurate** as Cassio's **abilities** as a **soldier** are called into **question** by the **play's events**. For example, when he's **stripped** of his **role as lieutenant**, he **persuades Desdemona** to take up his **cause** instead of **confronting Othello directly** which suggests that he can be **weak** and **cowardly**.

3) **In spite** of Cassio's **intellect**, Iago is able to **manipulate** him because Cassio only has "**bookish**" **intelligence** rather than **practical common sense** — he fails to see that Iago is **deceiving** him.

Cassio has a **Complex Relationship** with **Women**

In Oliver Parker's 1995 film, the character of Cassio forgets Bianca's name to show how little he thinks of her.

It's clear that Cassio **appeals** to **women** — he's "**a fellow almost damned in a fair wife**" (1.1.21). He uses **charming language** to **flatter** women, but he can be **cruel** and uses them for **selfish gain**.

He worships Desdemona...

• Cassio **praises** Desdemona using **exaggerated language** — he sees her as a **chaste goddess**: "**Hail to thee lady! And the grace of heaven, / Before, behind thee, and on every hand**" (2.1.85-86). He uses **religious language** to **elevate** Desdemona to a **divine level**: "**That paragons description and wild fame**" (2.1.62).

• He **refuses** to be **lured** into a **bawdy conversation** with Iago about the **consummation** of Othello and Desdemona's **marriage**. He simply says that Desdemona's a "**most exquisite lady**" (2.3.18).

He mocks Bianca...

• Cassio **treats** his **lover**, Bianca, with **contempt** and **mocks her** for her **affections**. Iago comments that when Cassio "**hears of her, [he] cannot refrain / From the excess of laughter**" (4.1.98-99).

• Cassio treats Bianca **kindly** when he's **alone** with her, calling her "**fair Bianca**" and "**sweet love**" (3.4.166-167). However he's **concerned** about being seen "**womaned**" (3.4.191) with her. He's a **hypocrite** because he's **happy** to **take advantage** of Bianca, but only if his **reputation remains intact**. Cassio's **more concerned** with having a **good appearance** than **actually treating** people with **genuine kindness**.

• Cassio's cruel **treatment** of Bianca could have something to do with her **lower-class status** or the fact that she's a **courtesan** — he places great **importance** on **class** and **rank**.

Cassio

He's **Concerned** with his **Appearance**

This is a concern shared by other characters e.g. Othello and Iago (see p.24 and p.27).

1) Cassio is **conscious** of how he **appears** to the **other characters**. He's very **concerned** with seeming **polite** and **respectable**: "Let it not gall your patience, good Iago, / That I extend my manners; 'tis my breeding" (2.1.97-98).

2) Cassio **loses** his **position** as Othello's **lieutenant** after a **drunken fight** with **Roderigo** and **Montano**. This fight is **provoked** by **slights** on Cassio's **reputation**:

   - Although Roderigo's **confrontation** with Cassio occurs **off-stage**, Roderigo agrees to take **Iago's advice** of "tainting [Cassio's] discipline" (2.1.259) — **questioning** his **reputation**.

   - Similarly, Cassio **starts** a **fight** with Montano because he **accuses** Cassio of being "drunk" (2.3.149). Cassio takes **offence** to this as he thinks that it's an **attack** on his **honour**.

3) Losing his position leaves Cassio **ashamed** and **embarrassed**: "Reputation, reputation, reputation! O, I have lost my reputation!" (2.3.255-256). His **repeated use** of the word "reputation" emphasises how **highly** he values it.

4) Cassio thinks that **reputation** and **honour** are **linked**, and like Othello, he thinks **military honour** is **important**. The thought of his **lost reputation** gives him **physical pain** — he says that it is "past all surgery" (2.3.253). He also says "I have lost the immortal part of myself and what remains is bestial" (2.3.256-257) which suggests that his **reputation** as a **soldier** has almost **spiritual significance**.

Cassio frequently uses hyperbole to exaggerate his feelings.

Iago Exploits Certain Aspects of Cassio's Character

1) Because Iago believes Cassio to be **intelligent**, Iago decides not to **outsmart** him in the **same obvious way** that he **manipulates foolish Roderigo**. Instead he **focuses** on the **weaknesses** in Cassio's character which he **can exploit**.

2) Iago **takes advantage** of the fact that Cassio:

   - **Can't hold his drink** — this is Cassio's **self-proclaimed weakness**: "I have very poor and unhappy brains for drinking" (2.3.30-31). He's a **violent drunk** because he's **not used to** drinking. This suggests that Cassio doesn't usually **join in** with **immoral behaviour**.

   - **Is weak** — Iago **easily persuades** Cassio to get **Desdemona** to take up **his cause** because Cassio's **reluctant** to face Othello himself — he's **worried** Othello will call him a "drunkard" (2.3.295). This helps **convince** Othello that Desdemona and Cassio are having an **affair**, as Desdemona is seen to be **showing** Cassio **favour**.

   - **Is charming** — Cassio's **youthful good looks** and **flirtatious behaviour** towards Emilia and Desdemona in Act 2, Scene 1 make it easy for Cassio "To be suspected, framed to make a woman false" (1.3.392). However, Cassio's **behaviour** is **presented** as entirely **innocent** — he seems to be **well-mannered**, **sincere** and **open**, even if he does go **over the top** sometimes.

3) In spite of his **weaknesses**, Cassio **replaces Othello** as **governor** at the **ending** of the play. It's **ironic** that Iago's **plots** to **dislodge Cassio** from a **position of power** actually lead to him **gaining** an even **higher role**. It seems **appropriate** that Cassio is given **responsibility** for "the censure of this hellish villain" (5.2.364).

Practice Questions

Q1 Some critics have argued that Cassio has an idea of himself as a gentleman, which can appear appropriate for his character or as something more calculated. Assess Cassio's opinion of himself in comparison to how the other characters view him. Back up your answer with examples from the text.

Q2 'All of Cassio's positive qualities are undermined by his unforgivable treatment of Bianca.' To what extent do you agree with this statement? Refer to the text in your answer.

Q3 'Cassio's exaggerated language is empty and meaningless.' How does Cassio's frequent use of hyperbole affect the audience's view of him? Back up your answer with examples from the text.

"For Michael Cassio, I dare be sworn I think that he is honest"

Iago's main criticism of Cassio is that he's an "arithmetician". This basically means that he's a thinker rather than a doer. Iago thinks Cassio should just stick to sums — he's so good at maths he might as well be a calculator. What do you mean, he already is...?

Emilia

Like the other women in the play Emilia is used by the male characters, but unlike the rest of other women she actually manages to strike back. It's Bard Wars Episode 5: Emilia Strikes Back, much better than Episode 1: The Ottoman Menace.

Emilia is **Loyal** to **Iago** and **Desdemona**

1) Emilia's marriage to Iago is **unhappy** — Iago doesn't **love** or **respect** her and **never shows** her **affection**. She's **critical** of **men** and **cynical** about **marriage**, but **remains loyal** to Iago:

© Johan Persson / ArenaPAL

- Emilia is so **desperate** for Iago's **affection** that she **betrays Desdemona** and **steals** her **handkerchief**: **"I nothing but to please his fantasy"** (3.3.296).
- Even though she's **trying** to **please Iago**, he shows her **little appreciation** and just **snatches** the handkerchief, telling Emilia **"leave me"** (3.3.317).
- Emilia **remains loyal** to Iago until the **end** of the play when she **discovers** his **treachery** and his **role** in **Desdemona's death**. She **acknowledges** a **duty** to **obey** her **husband**, but still **speaks out**: **"Tis proper I obey him, but not now"** (5.2.195).

2) Emilia is **loyal** to her **mistress** and even **sacrifices** her **life** to **clear Desdemona's name**. However, she **betrays Desdemona** when she **steals** her **handkerchief**.

Loyalty and Betrayal

Emilia **betrays** her **mistress** to **obey** her **husband**. She **only betrays** Desdemona **once**, by **stealing** the **handkerchief**, but it has **terrible consequences** — it **convinces** Othello of Desdemona's **infidelity** and he **murders** her. Emilia's **betrayal** is made **worse** by the fact that she **trusts Iago** with the handkerchief **without knowing why** he **wants it** — she knows that Desdemona will **"run mad"** (3.3.314) when she finds it's **missing**.

She's a **Foil** to **Desdemona**

A foil is a character who contrasts with one of the main characters but also shares key characteristics.

1) Emilia is a **foil** to Desdemona because they both have **troubled marriages**. They have a **strong relationship** which parallels the **close friendships** between the **military men** in *Othello*. Emilia also **shares some** of her **mistress's qualities**:

- Both are **loyal wives** who want to **please** and **obey their husbands**. Emilia **steals** the **handkerchief** because: **"My wayward husband hath a hundred times / Wooed me to steal it"** (3.3.289-290).
- Emilia and Desdemona **defend themselves**, and **womankind** against the **male characters** in the play. Desdemona **defends** Emilia **"Do not learn of him, Emilia, though he be thy husband"** (2.1.159), and Emilia **maintains** that **Desdemona** is **innocent** of **infidelity**.

2) Emilia is **more realistic** about **relationships** than Desdemona, and **believes** that **men** often **use women** like **objects** and then **discard them**. She says men **"are all but stomachs, and we but food"** (3.4.100), which suggests that she **doesn't believe** that **marriage** is based on **love** and **affection**. Emilia **blames men** for their wives' **unhappiness** whereas Desdemona **blames herself** for Othello's behaviour.

3) They also have **contrasting opinions** on **adultery** — Emilia **argues** that women have just as much **reason** to **cheat** as men, and if women are **unfaithful** it's **"their husbands' faults"**(4.3.85). Desdemona can't even **believe** that a woman would ever **cheat**. This also shows that Emilia's **morals** are not as **strict** as Desdemona's.

Emilia **Stands Up** for her **Mistress**

1) Emilia **defends Desdemona** as her mistress becomes **increasingly powerless** — she says she would **lay down [her] soul at stake"** to **"wager she is honest"** (4.2.11-12), and later even **sacrifices** her life to **prove** Desdemona's **innocence**.

2) She's also **perceptive** enough to realise that **"The Moor's abused by some most villainous knave"** (4.2.138) and eventually **reveals** Iago's **treachery**. By revealing Iago's **deception** she **confirms** Desdemona's **honesty**: **"she was chaste; she loved thee, cruel Moor"** (5.2.247).

3) Critics such as **Harold Bloom** argue that Emilia is the **only character** that Iago **underestimates**, and this is why she's **responsible** for his **downfall**. Ironically, Iago **fails** to **understand** the person he should have **known best** — his **wife**.

4) **In spite** of the **consequences**, Emilia **bravely defends** her **mistress**, and ensures that both Iago and Othello are **punished**. Iago **silences** Emilia for **betraying him** by **killing** her, even though it's **too late**.

Bianca

Bianca's a prostitute with a heart, but she has a pretty difficult time of it... It's kind of like the plot of 'Pretty Woman' — man hires prostitute, she falls in love with him, he treats her like dirt and — Hmmm. Maybe it's not so similar after all.

Bianca is **Defined** by her **Profession**

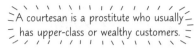
A courtesan is a prostitute who usually has upper-class or wealthy customers.

1) Bianca is a **courtesan** who lives in **Cyprus**. Her profession is **never explicitly stated** in the **play** but Shakespeare **heavily implies** it — this has been **debated** by critics such as **Edward Petcher**.

2) Cassio is Bianca's **favourite** "**customer**" (4.1.120). Bianca **falls in love** with him and the **idea** of **marrying him**. Unfortunately, Cassio **isn't serious** about her and sees her as a "**bauble**" (4.1.135) which shows that he thinks of her as a **pretty** but **insignificant object**.

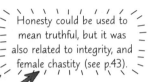
Honesty could be used to mean truthful, but it was also related to integrity, and female chastity (see p.43).

3) **Other characters** in the play assume that Bianca's **profession** as a **courtesan reflects** her **general moral character**. When Iago suggests that she was **involved** in the **attack** on Cassio, she **denies** it and says "**I am no strumpet; but of life as honest / As you that thus abuse me**" (5.1.122-123). Ironically, Bianca is **more honest** than her **accusers**, **Iago** and **Emilia**.

She's another **Foil** to **Desdemona**

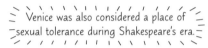
Venice was also considered a place of sexual tolerance during Shakespeare's era.

1) As a **courtesan**, Bianca is a **foil** to **Desdemona** who's **faithful**, **chaste** and **virtuous**. Othello doesn't see a **difference** in **morality** between the **two characters** — he calls Desdemona a "**whore**" and a "**strumpet**" (4.2.80 and 85). This shows how much he's been **influenced** by Iago's **misogyny**.

2) Desdemona and Bianca are both **accused** of being **promiscuous**, but there's **nothing** in the **play** to **prove** that either of them were **disloyal** to their **lovers**, and both appear to **genuinely love** their partners. Bianca exclaims "**my dear Cassio! my sweet Cassio!**" (5.1.76) when she **discovers** that he's been **injured**, and Desdemona greets her husband as "**My dear Othello**" (2.1.176).

3) Like Desdemona, Bianca is **defined** by her **relationship with men** and is **used** by her lover before being **discarded**. Cassio doesn't even want to be **seen with her**, refusing to let Othello see him "**womaned**" (3.4.191).

4) Bianca is of a **lower class** than Desdemona, so she's in a **vulnerable position** in society. **Ironically**, despite being the **least powerful figure** in the play, she's the **only female character** to **survive**.

She **Shares Similarities** with **Othello**

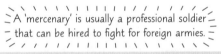
A 'mercenary' is usually a professional soldier that can be hired to fight for foreign armies.

1) Like Othello, Bianca could be said to be **a mercenary** — her **profession** involves **working** for **whoever's willing to pay** for her services. This is **similar** to Othello's **profession**, except he is paid to **fight** rather than to **love**. They could both also be **described** as **outsiders** who are **shunned** and **mistreated** by **other characters**.

2) Both Othello and Bianca suffer from **jealousy** about their **lovers** — their **suspicions** are **caused** by the **handkerchief**. Cassio comments that Bianca is "**jealous**" (3.4.181) and Bianca's **language illustrates** her **anger**: "**I was a fine fool to take it... This is some minx's token, and I must take out the work?**" (4.1.150-153).

3) They also **react differently** to jealousy — Othello turns to "**savage madness**" (4.1.55) whereas Bianca gives Cassio a **chance** to **explain** himself: "**you'll come to supper tonight**" (4.1.159) and **continues** to **love him**.

Practice Questions

Q1 'Iago's view of women is that they are foolish, weak-minded and unfaithful'.
Assess whether any of the female characters in the play give Iago cause to make such a judgement.

Q2 Some critics argue that Emilia suspects Iago throughout the play, but doesn't react until it's too late because of her feelings towards her husband. Make a case arguing both for and against this idea. Refer to the text in your answer.

"What should such a fool / Do with so good a wife?"

It seems as if the men in 'Othello' don't deserve the love and loyalty of their lovers... Luckily most of them get their just desserts: Iago ends up in the custard whilst Othello ends up eating Devil's Food Cake — it's all because they treated their women like tarts...

Roderigo

An anagram of Roderigo is 'Order, I go' — which pretty much sums up his relationship with Iago.
Roderigo's another victim of Iago's scheming, but his unpleasantness means that there's not much pity for him...

Roderigo is Rich and Foolish

Roderigo is a **rich**, **jealous Venetian** who is in **love** with Desdemona. Iago exploits his **feelings** and calls him the **"poor trash of Venice"** (2.1.294). Shakespeare **presents** him as a **foolish**, **ignorant character**:

© Johan Persson / Arena PAL

- He's **easily manipulated** and Iago **quickly recognises** this: **"Thus do I ever make my fool my purse"** (1.3.377). Iago constantly **controls** him and Roderigo relies on Iago to **direct his actions**, repeatedly asking **"What should I do?"** (1.3.314).
- He's **rejected** by Desdemona — he's one of the **"wealthy curlèd darlings"** (1.2.68) that **failed** to **win** her. He **continues** to **pursue** her even **after** she **marries Othello**.
- He's **superficial** and thinks that he can **buy Desdemona's love**. He sees a **direct relationship** between **expensive gifts** and **love**: **"The jewels you have had from me to deliver Desdemona would half have corrupted a votarist"** (4.2.186-188).

Roderigo is One of Iago's Victims

Roderigo can be seen as a villain, a victim or both.

1) He's Iago's **first victim** in the play — he's an **easy target** for Iago's **deviousness**:

- His **belief** that **money and jewels** will **win Desdemona** means that it's **easy** for Iago to persuade him to **"provide [his] money"** (1.3.366) even when there's **no sign** that Desdemona has **feelings** for him.
- Iago **takes advantage** of Roderigo's **love** for Desdemona to **use him** to **destroy Cassio**. Iago **promises** Roderigo **"a shorter journey to your desires"** if he **provokes a fight** with Cassio (2.1.268).
- Once Roderigo has **outlived his usefulness**, Iago decides to **get rid of him** — his **death** is the result of being **stabbed in the back** by Iago. He uses Roderigo's **death** to **conveniently shift** the blame onto **him**.

2) Roderigo **realises** that Iago is **manipulating him**, and **knows** that Iago **says one thing** but then **does another**: **"your words and performances are no kin together"** (4.2.182-183). However, he still does **Iago's bidding**, which suggests that he's a **villain** as well as a **victim**. Roderigo shares **many characteristics** with Iago:

- both are **racist** — Roderigo **mirrors** Iago's **racist language** and calls Othello a **"lascivious Moor"** (1.1.127).
- both are **immoral** — Iago **easily convinces** Roderigo to **provoke Brabantio's anger** and to **kill Cassio**, even though he has **"no great devotion to the deed"** (5.1.8). **Neither** of them have **any sense** of **morality**.
- both **create disorder** and chaos in the play — Iago is a **malevolent destructive force** throughout the play, and he **encourages** Roderigo to be the **same in Act 5, Scene 1**. However, Roderigo continues to **act** on Iago's **directions** rather than **creating evil himself** — Iago is far more **devious** and **cunning** than **foolish** Roderigo.

Iago's **manipulation** of Roderigo also allows the **audience** a **glimpse** into **Iago's mind** because he's **more open** in his **interactions** with Roderigo than with **any other character**.

He Provides a Contrast to Othello

Whilst Othello is a **great man** whose life ends in **tragedy**, Roderigo's **foolishness** provides **comedy** because his **behaviour** is **ridiculous**. However, there are several **parallels** between Othello and Roderigo:

1) Both men **love Desdemona**, but Othello **successfully woos her**. Despite Roderigo's **foolishness**, Brabantio says he would **rather** see Desdemona **marry Roderigo** than a **black man**: **"O, would you had had her!"** (1.1.176).

2) Like Othello, Roderigo is an **outsider** in the sense that Iago **keeps him away** from **others** to make sure he can **completely control** him. However, Roderigo helps to **reinforce** the idea that Othello is an **outsider** — he's a **racist** and helps **shape** Brabantio's **negative perceptions** of Othello.

3) Roderigo's also a **victim** of the **"green-eyed monster"** (3.3.164) of **jealousy**, like Othello. This shows that jealousy is a **universal emotion** — it can be felt by **anyone regardless** of their **class**, **gender** or **race**.

4) Roderigo, like Othello, is **ignorant** of Iago's **deception** until it's **too late**: **"O damned Iago!"** (5.1.62). This shows that Iago **can deceive fools** like Roderigo, as well as **noble**, **powerful men** like Othello.

Brabantio

Brabantio's one of the first characters to appear in 'Othello'. He's an important senator and he's Desdemona's father so you'd think he'd have a big role in the play... Except, he's only in Act 1, and he's dead by the end of Act 5. Ho hum...

Brabantio is Desdemona's Father

1) Brabantio is an **important Venetian senator** as well as **Desdemona's father**. He's **highly regarded** as a senator, and the Duke says that he missed his **"counsel and your help"** (1.3.51) during their discussion of the Turkish fleet. He **expects people** to **listen** to him and has a **high opinion** of his **own importance**.

2) Brabantio feels that he **deserves respect** as the **head** of his **family**. In the **Elizabethan era**, the **father** often **chose** his **daughter's husband**, but Brabantio is **initially** quite **liberal** — he **allows Desdemona** to **reject suitors** that were thought to be **"The wealthy curlèd darlings of our nation"** (1.2.68).

3) When Desdemona goes **behind his back** and marries **outside** of her **race**, he's **outraged** and **disowns her**.

He's Upset by Desdemona's Actions

> Brabantio feels betrayed when Othello marries Desdemona. He places the first seed of doubt about Desdemona's fidelity: "She has deceived her father, and may thee" (1.3.290).

1) Brabantio is **obviously shocked** by Desdemona's **behaviour** — he thought that Desdemona was **"A maiden never bold"** (1.3.94). In light of Desdemona's **actions**, this suggests that he **didn't know** his daughter very well.

2) Brabantio **responds emotionally** to her **actions** — at **first** he seems **desperate** and **exasperated**, asking **bewildered questions** like **"Who would be a father?"** (1.1.165). He then becomes **furious** about his daughter's **betrayal**, declaring **"I had rather adopt a child than get it"** (1.3.189), and calling Othello a **"foul thief"** (1.2.62).

3) Initially the **loss** of his daughter might make the audience **sympathise** with Brabantio, but his **excessive grief** begins to make him seem **comical**. The way that Brabantio **treats Desdemona** like a **possession**, calling Othello a **"thief"** (1.2.62) and Desdemona a **"jewel"** (1.3.193), also makes him seem **less sympathetic**.

4) Brabantio also loses the **audience's sympathy** by using **racist language** — he says to Othello that Desdemona has gone **"to the sooty bosom / Of such a thing as thou"** (1.2.70).

5) Brabantio's **angry language contrasts** with Othello's **eloquent** and **balanced speech**. Brabantio uses **exaggerated words** such as **"o'erbearing"** and **"engluts"** (1.3.56-57) which make him **appear absurd** — he's **so emotional** that the other senators think Desdemona is **dead** (1.3.59).

6) Ultimately, Brabantio is **so affected** by Desdemona's **marriage** that he **dies shortly** after: the **"match was mortal to him, and pure grief / Shore his old thread in twain"** (5.2.204-205).

He holds Prejudiced Views

1) Othello claims that Brabantio: **"loved me, oft invited me"** (1.3.127) to spend time in his **home**. However, Brabantio **doesn't think** that Othello is a **suitable suitor** for his daughter, and **refuses** to **accept** her **marriage** to a **Moor**.

2) Brabantio is a **racist**, claiming that the **only reason** Desdemona would **marry Othello** is if he had **"practised on her with foul charms"** (1.2.73). He also says that their **interracial marriage** is **"Against all rules of nature"** (1.3.101).

3) Some critics suggest that Brabantio's **racist view** of Othello was **shaped** by Iago and Roderigo — he could be seen as a **victim** as he **can't distinguish** between **appearance** and **reality** (see p.43). This is shown when he describes **Desdemona** as a **"maiden never bold"** who should have **"feared to look"** on Othello (1.3.94 and 98).

Practice Questions

Q1 'Roderigo is a much more sympathetic character than Brabantio'.
To what extent do you agree with this statement? Give examples from the text in your answer.

Q2 Gratiano claims Brabantio's death was caused by grief over Desdemona's marriage. Do you think that it could be argued that Brabantio's death was more likely caused by a loss of pride and reputation? Refer to the text in your answer.

"Poor Desdemona! I am glad thy father's dead: / Thy match was mortal to him"

Brabantio Brabantio Brabantio — if you say it quickly and repeatedly it kind of sounds like an old fashioned steam train rolling up and down on the tracks. Please don't say it's just me. Coincidentally both Brabantio and steam engines are full of hot air...

Jealousy

Poor Cassio — everyone seems to be jealous of him and he hasn't even done anything wrong. He just has that lovely hair, that sexy twinkle in his eye, that boyish charm... Come to think of it, I'd stab him in the leg too given half a chance.

Jealousy is a **Powerful** and **Destructive Force**

1) Jealousy drives most of the **action** in *Othello* — **Iago's** jealousy prompts him to **ruin** Cassio's **career** and Othello's **happiness**, and **Othello's** jealousy causes him to **destroy** his **marriage**, **kill** his **wife** and eventually **kill himself**.

2) Jealousy is **destructive** because it's **irrational**: "jealous souls [...] are not ever jealous for the cause" (3.4.155-156). This means that it quickly spirals **out of control**, leading to **violence**, **murder** and the **loss** of people's **good qualities**, e.g. Othello's **nobility**.

3) Jealousy makes people **lose** their **judgement**, so "**Trifles**" become "**strong / As proofs of holy writ**" (3.3.319-321). Although Othello **demands proof**, he **readily accepts** the **handkerchief** as **firm evidence** of Desdemona's infidelity.

'Othello and Desdemona' by Daniel Maclise (1859)

Photo © Christie's Images

Iago experiences **Professional Jealousy**

1) Iago is jealous that **Cassio** has been **promoted** to Othello's **lieutenant**, for several reasons:

- He believes that he should have been promoted **instead** of Cassio: "**I know my price, I am worth no worse a place.**" (1.1.11). As Othello's 'ancient' he holds a fairly **low position**, yet feels superior to Cassio. Cassio's promotion **undermines** his sense of **superiority**, so he tries to **regain his dominance** by plotting against others.

- He believes that Cassio is a "**great arithmetician**" (1.1.19) with **no practical experience** of warfare, whereas Iago has fought alongside Othello "**At Rhodes, at Cyprus, and on other grounds**" (1.1.29). He's **bitter** that "**proof**" (1.1.28) of his **good service** has been overlooked, and **questions** Othello's **judgement**.

- Iago also has a **chip on his shoulder** about the reasons for Cassio's promotion: "**Preferment goes by letter and affection**" (1.1.36) — Iago is **angry** that **success** seems based on **favouritism**, rather than **ability**.

2) Iago's **jealousy** of Cassio's success leads him to try to **destroy** Cassio's **career**. Even after Cassio has been **sacked**, Iago **punishes** him further by persuading Othello that Cassio has **seduced** Desdemona.

3) Iago's **persistence** in scheming to hurt Cassio, even when he seems to have **little reason**, has led some critics to argue that his jealousy is **merely one** of **many excuses** to create **disorder** (see p.26).

Sexual Jealousy springs from **Love** and **Insecurity**

1) The **strength** of Othello's **jealousy** arises in part from the strength of his **love**. He loves Desdemona "**not wisely, but too well**" (5.2.340) — when he begins to suspect that she is **unfaithful**, this passion **changes** from love to jealousy.

2) Othello's **sexual jealousy** is fuelled by **insecurity**. In Act 3, Scene 3 he cites his **race** and **age** as reasons that Desdemona might cheat on him. Iago plays on Othello's **insecurities** to convince him that Desdemona is **unfaithful**:

- He knows that Othello is **inexperienced** with Venetian women (see p.55).

- He argues that Desdemona "**did deceive her father, marrying you**" (3.3.204), and links her to the **dishonest** Venetian women who care only that their antics remain "**unknown**" (3.3.202).

- He plays on Othello's **racial insecurity** by suggesting that Desdemona will eventually **compare** Othello with "**her country forms**" and "**repent**" of her marriage to him (3.3.235-236).

3) Initially Othello **refuses** to believe Iago, saying that his own "**weak merits**" (3.3.185) **aren't** proof of Desdemona's infidelity. However, Iago's skilful **manipulation** of Othello's insecurities quickly drives him to jealousy.

4) Sexual jealousy is also linked to men's **reputation** (see p.39) and **masculinity**. Othello claims that Desdemona's betrayal makes him "**a monster and a beast**" (4.1.62), suggesting that he's been humiliated as a **cuckold** (see p.39).

Iago's Motives

Iago is jealous of Cassio's **honest** and **attractive personality**, believing that Cassio's "**daily beauty [...] makes me ugly**" (5.1.19). Iago has also heard **rumours** that Othello "'**twixt my sheets / [Has] done my office**" (1.3.381-382). Iago admits that he has **no evidence** — "**I know not if't be true**" (1.3.382) — yet **acts** on his **suspicions** anyway. Iago's **unsubstantiated claims** suggest that **sexual jealousy** is just an **excuse** to **cause trouble**.

Jealousy

Shakespeare presents Jealousy as Consuming and Unnatural

1) Characters who suffer from jealousy are **consumed** by it, and **cannot think rationally**. Iago describes Othello as **"eaten up with passion"** (3.3.388), and says that the thought of Emilia's **infidelity "Doth, like a poisonous mineral, gnaw my inwards"** (2.1.288).

Iago links jealousy to poison again when he says he will "pour this pestilence into [Othello's] ear" (2.3.346).

2) Shakespeare associates the **effects** of jealousy with the imagery of **hell**: **"Arise, black vengeance, from the hollow hell!"** (3.3.444). This suggests that jealousy isn't just a **dangerous primal** force, but it's also an **evil** one.

3) Emilia describes jealousy as a **"monster / Begot upon itself, born on itself"** (3.4.157-158) — jealousy **grows** by **feeding on itself**. Shakespeare develops this **metaphor** of jealousy as a **monster**:

Context
The Greek poet **Sappho** connected **green** with **envy** in 7 BC, when she used it to describe a **forgotten lover**. Shakespeare made the link between **green** and **jealousy** much more **explicit**.

O, beware, my lord, of jealousy!
It is the green-eyed monster, which doth mock
The meat it feeds on.

(3.3.163-165)

Language
The word **"mock"** reminds the audience of **Iago's** habit of taking **pleasure** in the other characters' misfortunes. This connects him to the **"monster"**, making him a **personification** of **jealousy**.

Imagery
Shakespeare introduces the idea of jealousy as a **monster**, which **eats up** the **"meat"** of the person who experiences it. The word **"feeds"** suggests that jealousy is a **consuming force**.

It's Debatable whether Othello becomes jealous Too Easily

1) At the end of the play Othello describes himself as **"one not easily jealous, but being wrought / Perplexed in the extreme"** (5.2.341-342), as he tries to restore his nobility. Othello emphasises that the circumstances that Iago created were **extreme** — arguably **any man** would have fallen into **jealousy** in the same **position**.

2) The view of Othello as **"not easily jealous"** is **supported** and **contradicted** by the play — he **doesn't** given in to jealousy **immediately**, and says that Desdemona **"loves company"** which is a **"virtue"** (3.3.182-184). He trusts her because **"she had eyes and chose me"** (3.3.187), demanding **"ocular proof"** (3.3.357) before he will believe her **guilt**.

3) However, it only takes **seeing Cassio** with the **handkerchief** for Othello to **believe** that Desdemona is **unfaithful**. Iago **convinces** Othello of Desdemona's guilt **fairly easily**. Othello's **transformation** in Act 3, Scene 3 happens in a **long** and **intense scene** which makes it seem like **time** is **passing quickly**, **emphasising** the **speed** of his **downfall**.

4) Desdemona **refuses** to believe that Othello is jealous: **"the sun where he was born / Drew all such humours from him"** (3.4.30-31). The audience sees the **dramatic irony** of this, and questions how well she really knows him.

5) Bianca acts as a **foil** to Othello, allowing Shakespeare to show an **alternative** response to jealousy. When she suspects that Cassio is cheating on her, she gives him a **chance** to explain or redeem himself: **"If you'll come to supper tonight, you may"** (4.1.159). This hints at the path that Othello could have chosen, making his **downfall** more **tragic**.

Symbolism — the handkerchief
Both Othello and Bianca see the **handkerchief** as a **symbol** of their partner's **infidelity**. It was **originally** a symbol of Othello's **love** for Desdemona, but comes to represent her '**betrayal**', which shows how jealousy can **transform** a **positive** symbol into a **negative** one. The fact that Othello is **convinced** of Desdemona's **betrayal** by such an **insubstantial object** highlights how **irrational** jealousy is.

Practice Questions

Q1 'Without jealousy, there would be no play.' To what extent do you agree with this view of *Othello*?

Q2 'None of the characters in *Othello* have any cause for jealousy, yet most of them experience it.' To what extent do you agree with this statement? Back up your answer with examples from the text.

"It is the green-eyed monster, which doth mock / The meat it feeds on"

I like to mock the meat I feed on, it makes me feel better about eating it. "Pleased to meat you", "Arise, Sir Loin" — that kind of thing. I tried to branch out into vegetables too, but somehow calling a bowl of salad "wet lettuce" just made me feel like a loser.

Gender and Sexuality

Well, it's like this you see... Sometimes when a mummy bird really loves a daddy bird and, um, there are some bees nearby... What's that? It's a book about 'Othello'? Thank God, I thought it was PSHE.

Gender played an Important role in Elizabethan Society

Ironically, for most of Shakespeare's life, there was a woman on the throne.

1) In Elizabethan times, men held most of the power both in **society** and in their **relationships** with women.

Men
- Society was **patriarchal** — this meant **men** had **more power** in society and over their own **families**, while women were expected to **obey** them. In *Othello*, Brabantio is **shocked** that his daughter has **gone against** his wishes by marrying Othello, and asks her where she "**owe[s] obedience**" (1.3.178). When Desdemona replies that her "**duty**" is "**to the Moor**" (1.3.184-187) rather than to her father, he **disowns** her.
- **Men** were **expected** to **act** rather than **talk**, and **honour** and **reputation** were very important. Othello defines himself as a **soldier**, boasting that "**little of this great world can I speak / More than pertains to feats of broil and battle**" (1.3.86-87). Iago **criticises** Cassio for being like a "**spinster**" because he's seen **so little action** on the **battlefield** — he's "**prattle without practice**" (1.1.24-26).

2) **Women** were considered to be **socially**, **intellectually** and **physically inferior** to men.

Women
- It was still an **accepted idea** that women were **responsible** for humanity's **fall into evil**, based on **Eve's** role in the Bible. Since classical times, women had been considered to be '**faulty**' versions of men.
- Women were **dependent** on their **father** till they **married**, when they became dependent on their **husband**.
- Women had to be **virgins** before **marriage** to ensure their children were legitimate — men needed to make sure that any **property** was **inherited** by their **biological sons** and not **illegitimate heirs**.
- Women were seen as either **chaste** and **pure**, or **promiscuous**. If a woman was **unfaithful**, she made a '**cuckold**' of her husband (see p.39), destroyed his "**good name**" (3.3.158) and **masculine reputation**.

Men in 'Othello' try to Control Women

1) **Women** are repeatedly referred to as if they are the '**property**' of the male characters. Iago tells Brabantio that he has been "**robbed**" (1.1.87) of Desdemona, putting her in the same category as Brabantio's "**house**" and "**bags**" (1.1.81). Brabantio continues this, addressing Othello as a "**foul thief**" (1.2.62) and Desdemona as a "**jewel**" (1.3.193).

2) Othello treats Desdemona as an **equal** in the **early** stages of the play, but when he suspects she's **unfaithful**, he tries to **reassert** his **control** over her both **verbally** and **physically**. He mourns his **lack of control** over her behaviour: "**we can call these delicate creatures ours / And not their appetites!**" (3.3.266-267).

3) Cassio expects Bianca to **obey** him, using **orders** to speak to **her**: "**Take it, and do't, and leave me**" (3.4.187). He sees her as an **insignificant object** — a "**bauble**" (4.1.135).

4) Iago **controls** Emilia's behaviour, giving her **instructions** which Emilia **obeys**, even though this **conflicts** with her **loyalty** to Desdemona (e.g. when she steals the handkerchief).

'Desdemona Kneeling at her Father's Feet' by Eugene Delacroix (1852)

© The Art Archive / Musée Saint Denis Reims / Gianni Dagli Orti

The Female characters Break some of society's Conventions

1) Desdemona **breaks convention** by marrying a black man in secret, **against** her father's wishes. By **taking up** Cassio's cause with Othello, she tries to **control** her **husband's actions**, **inverting** their **gender roles** (see p.28).

Desdemona and Gender

Othello's claim that Desdemona "**wished / That heaven had made her such a man**" (1.3.161-162) is **ambiguous**. On the surface she is wishing for a **husband** like Othello, but the line could also be read as her wishing that she had been **born a man**. This is supported by her eager desire to "**go to war**" (1.3.253) with Othello, and **masculine descriptions** of her as a "**general**" (2.3.306) and "**our great Captain's Captain**" (2.1.74).

2) As a **courtesan**, Bianca is seen as **promiscuous** and **dishonest**. However, she **challenges** expectations by being more **honest** than Cassio, who abuses her behind her back. Later, she claims to be "**as honest**" as Emilia (5.1.122).

3) When Emilia learns of Iago's **scheming**, she goes against her **husband**: "'**Tis proper I obey him — but not now**" (5.2.195). When Iago realises that he can no longer **control** Emilia, he **silences** her by **killing** her.

Gender and Sexuality

The **Male** characters feel **Threatened** by **Female Sexuality**

1) Not all **female sexuality** is **troubling** in the play — for example, in **marriage**, men **celebrate** it.   Othello says "**the fruits are to ensue. / That profit's yet to come 'tween me and you**" (2.3.9-10), implying that **sex** is a **profit** of **marriage**.

2) However, the **men** in the play do feel **threatened** by women **asserting themselves** through **sex**, i.e. by having **affairs** and being **promiscuous**. This might be because it could upset the **balance of power** in the **patriarchy**. ⟶ *In 'Othello' all three female characters are accused of infidelity, but there's no evidence that any of them have been unfaithful.*

3) **Many** of the **men voice** their **concerns** about **female sexuality** by **accusing** women of being **prostitutes**. Iago sees all women as **promiscuous**: "**you go to bed to work**" (2.1.114). When Othello thinks Desdemona has been **unfaithful**, he calls her a "**whore**" and "**strumpet**" (4.2.80 and 84) and describes Emilia as the "**mistress**" of a brothel (4.2.26).

4) In the sixteenth century, Venice was well known for its **loose morals** and large number of **courtesans**. This feeds into the male characters' **assumption** that the female characters are **promiscuous**. Iago takes **advantage** of Othello's **inexperience** with **Venetian women** to suggest they're all unfaithful and that he's a **cuckold**:

> **Cuckoldry**
>
> A cuckold is a **man** who has an **unfaithful wife**, but is the **last person** to **find out**. This is represented by **metaphorical horns** which **everyone** can **see** but him: "**a hornèd man's a monster and a beast**" (4.1.62). This was considered humiliating and the idea of being a "**monster**" and a "**beast**" is **dehumanising**. Othello shouts "**Cuckold me!**"(4.1.199) as if he **cannot believe** that he would be a **cuckold**.

5) There was a **double standard** about **infidelity** for men and women which Emilia **questions** — she points out that men "**pour our treasures into foreign laps**" and "**change us for others**" (4.3.87 and 96), without any **consequences** whilst adulterous women are **punished** by **men** and society. She **blames** the husbands "**if wives do fall**" (4.3.86).

Some **Relationships** are **Not Socially Acceptable**

1) Othello and Desdemona's **relationship** is **rejected** by some of the other characters:

   - **Brabantio** is shocked by the match because Othello is **black**, and believes that Othello must have used "**spells and medicines**" (1.3.61) to make Desdemona love him.
   - **Iago** calls it a "**frail vow betwixt an erring barbarian and a super-subtle Venetian**" (1.3.350-351).
   - Iago **plays on** Brabantio's fear of the match by referring to their sexual relationship in **bestial** terms: "**an old black ram / Is tupping your white ewe!**" (1.1.89-90).

   White is associated with goodness and innocence, whereas black is associated with sin and evil.

2) However, their marriage is **widely accepted** because of Othello's standing in the army. The **Duke** sanctions it because Othello's **virtues** make him "**more fair than black**" (1.3.287).

3) **Other relationships** were also presented as **socially unacceptable** — Iago's **behaviour** has led some **critics** to suggest that he's **homosexual**. For example, he describes an invented **erotic dream** in unnecessary **detail**: "**[Cassio] would kiss me hard [...] lay his leg o'er my thigh**" (3.3.419-422). Though Iago doesn't say so explicitly, it does provide a **possible motivation** for wanting to **destroy** Othello's marriage.

4) Although it would have been **common** for men in Elizabethan times to **visit prostitutes**, it was **unlikely** that they would make the **relationship public**. This is **illustrated** in the play by the way that **Cassio** is **happy** to **spend time** with **Bianca** and **treats** her **kindly** when they're **alone**, but in **public** he doesn't want Othello to see him with her.

Practice Questions

Q1 'Desdemona is a naive idealist when it comes to relationships, whereas Emilia is a realist'. To what extent do you agree with this statement? Give examples from the text in your answer.

Q2 In what ways are Othello and Iago's views of women similar, and how do they differ?

"I do think it is their husbands' faults / If wives do fall"

If you're writing about gender and sexuality have a think about the three female characters and how they're treated by men. It's interesting that Bianca, the prostitute, is the only one to survive. There's a moral in there somewhere, I'm just not sure what it is...

Love and War

War may play a pretty big part in the play, but I'll tell you one thing — it doesn't do a great deal for Othello's love life...

The **Male** characters **Define** themselves as **Soldiers**

This was one of Rymer's main objections to Iago's character (see p.56).

1) **Othello** has been a **soldier** since the age of **seven**, and defines himself by his **"dearest action"** (1.3.85) on the **battlefield**, and by his **ancestors**, who were **"men of royal siege"** (1.2.22). It **elevates** his **status** in **Venetian society** — the Venetians call him the **"warlike Moor"** and **"brave Othello"** (2.1.27 and 38).

2) **Iago** claims to be a **seasoned soldier**, who has fought **"At Rhodes, at Cyprus and on other grounds"** (1.1.29). Othello seems to **trust** Iago above Desdemona because soldiers were **traditionally** seen as **loyal** and **honest**.

3) Although he's **inexperienced** in battle, **Cassio** puts **great importance** on military **honour**, and is **devastated** at **losing** his position as Othello's **lieutenant**, which he describes as a hurt **"past all surgery"** (2.3.253). When the male characters feel like their honour is being **challenged**, their response is to engage in **conflict**.

4) The men's **shared military background** strengthens their **friendship**. Othello, Iago and Cassio openly declare their **love** for one another, and it wouldn't have been **surprising** that Iago and Cassio **shared a bed** (3.3.410-423), as this was a **common occurrence** in Elizabethan times.

Female friendships are also important — Desdemona confides in Emilia rather than her husband, and Emilia sacrifices her own life to defend Desdemona's honour.

Love is a **Powerful Force** in 'Othello'

1) *Othello* is a **domestic tragedy** so the focus is on **personal relationships** rather than the **politics** of **war**. **Love affects** and **motivates** many of the **characters** in the play.

2) Some characters are **positively affected** by love — it makes **Othello very happy**, **"It stops me here, it is too much of joy"** (2.1.191), while Iago comments that **"base men being in love have then a nobility in their natures"** (2.1.209-210).

3) Other characters are **negatively affected** by love — it can be **destructive** and **dangerous**:

- It makes people **irrational** — Roderigo's **love** for **Desdemona** turns him **"wrong side out"** (2.3.49), leads him to **follow Iago** and **ultimately causes** his **downfall**. Emilia's **betrayal** of Desdemona, **stealing** the **handkerchief**, is also **motivated** by her **unquestioning desire** to **"please [Iago's] fantasy"** (3.3.296).

- Both Desdemona and Othello are **naive** about **love** — Desdemona hopes that **"our loves and comforts should increase / Even as our days do grow"** (2.1.188-189) and Othello says that **"Chaos is come again"** when their **love** is **over** (3.3.92). They put **all** their **hopes** for **happiness** in **marriage**, which makes the **breakdown** so **tragic**.

The Battle of Lepanto in 1571, by J-F. Michaud (1877)

© Ken Welsh

This was a major victory for the Holy League (a group of Catholic states, including Venice) over the Turks.

Love and **War** seem **Compatible** at first...

1) Love and war are **combined** from the **beginning** of Othello and Desdemona's **relationship**. Othello explains **elegantly** that his tales of **war** caused Desdemona to **love** him: **"She loved me for the dangers I had passed"** (1.3.166). Desdemona seems to find his **military prowess attractive**, which is one of the reasons Othello **loves her back** — it makes him **feel heroic**. This implies that love and war can exist **harmoniously**.

2) Shakespeare uses the **imagery** of war to reveal the **strengths** of Othello and Desdemona's relationship:

- Desdemona pleads to go to Cyprus with Othello. Her passionate claim of **"downright violence and storm of fortunes"** (1.3.246) makes her seem **strong-willed** and **unafraid** — the **perfect match** for Othello.

- In **Cyprus**, Othello describes Desdemona as a **"fair warrior"** (2.1.176), suggesting that he values both her **beauty** and her **strength** of character. This implies that they are **well-matched**.

3) However, there are early **hints** that love will be **disrupted** by war — the Duke tells Othello that he must **"slubber [sully] the gloss of your new fortunes with this more stubborn and boisterous expedition"** (1.3.224-226).

4) Othello's speech in **Act 1, Scene 3** places war **before** love — he tells the senators that he will not **"your serious and great business scant / For she is with me"**, and calls the things of love **"light-winged toys"** (1.3.264-265). He's happy to leave for Cyprus **immediately**, even though it **physically separates** him from Desdemona, and uses **domestic imagery** to refer to his time at **war**, saying that **"the flinty and steel couch of war"** has become a **"bed of down"** (1.3.228-229).

Love and War

When *War Ends*, the *Conflict Shifts* to Othello's *Marriage*

1) When the characters reach Cyprus, the focus of the play shifts. Beforehand, there's a focus on **conflict** and the threat of **invasion** from the Turks. When the Turks **drown** and the "**wars are done**" (2.1.20), the focus shifts to the characters' **personal relationships**.

2) Othello and Desdemona's first night together in Cyprus is **interrupted** by **conflict**. This is an **ominous reminder** to the audience that Desdemona has chosen a life where "**strife**" will frequently interrupt the **couple's** "**balmy slumbers**" (2.3.251).

3) Othello's **self-esteem** is based on his military **honour** — it's one of the reasons that Desdemona fell in **love** with him: "**to his honours... / Did I my soul and fortunes consecrate**" (1.3.250-251). Once the **conflict** is over, Othello **initially continues** to **uphold** his **military honour**. He brings **order** after Cassio's **fight** and is the **voice** of **reason** and **morality**, reminding them of "**Christian shame**" and calling the brawl "**barbarous**" (2.3.166).

4) He's also concerned with ensuring that Cyprus is **safe** and inspects the "**fortifications**" (3.2.5). This creates **dramatic irony**, as the audience knows that these fortifications **won't** protect Othello's **marriage** from Iago's **attacks**.

> Iago effectively **wages war** on Othello. Early in the play he declares that he will "**show out a flag and sign of love**" (1.1.157) to convince Othello that he's **faithful**. In **military** terms, a **flag** is a sign of **loyalty** or **surrender** — in Iago's case it is "**indeed but sign**" (1.1.158), helping him to gain Othello's **trust** whilst working to **destroy** him.

The play's setting is significant. Cyprus was the birthplace of Aphrodite, the Greek goddess of love. Early in the play we learn that it is now a place of conflict, suggesting that war has replaced love as the dominant force there.

Love and *War* are ultimately *Incompatible*

1) At the beginning of the play, Iago describes Othello as being "**stuffed with epithets of war**" (1.1.14) — Othello's **life** before he marries Desdemona has been **focused** on matters of **war**.

2) Othello's **honour** and **military career** are so **integral** to his **character**, that when he becomes **convinced** of his wife's **infidelity**, he sees it as a **failure** of his **personal masculine honour**:

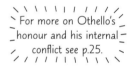

For more on Othello's honour and his internal conflict see p.25.

> In Othello's speech in **Act 3, Scene 3**, he starts to **merge** his **identities** as a **soldier** and **lover**, and reveals a **preoccupation** with his **own reputation**. He idealises the "**pomp and circumstance of glorious war**" and links Desdemona's **infidelity** with a **loss** of **honour**. He **bids farewell** to his **military career** and compares the loss of his wife to the loss of his **military prowess**: "**Othello's occupation's gone**" (3.3.351-354). He seems to **regret** that Desdemona has **replaced** his **military career** as a source of **honour**.

3) When Othello murders Desdemona, it shows that he's acting as a **soldier** once again — he claims that he **killed** her to defend his honour, justifying it by saying "**naught I did in hate, but all in honour**" (5.2.292) and calling himself a "**honourable murderer**" (5.2.291). His **sense** of **honour** is **stronger** than his **faith** in his **wife's innocence**. It could be that his **sense** of **honour** has been **tainted** by Iago — in Act 5, Scene 1, he says that Iago has a "**noble sense**" of right and wrong and that he "**teachest**" Othello how to act (5.1.32-33).

4) Othello's **final actions** emphasise his **military background** and he asks Lodovico to remember him as someone who has "**done the state some service**". At the end of the play, when Othello talks about his "**soldier's thigh**" (5.2.259), he seems to see himself as a **soldier** once again. He recognises his **failure** as a **lover** because he didn't love "**wisely**" and was "**perplexed**" by jealousy and **realises** that he "**threw a pearl away**" (5.2.335-343). As a soldier, the only **honourable** course of action left to Othello is to **die on his own sword**.

Practice Questions

Q1 Othello describes himself as "one that loved not wisely, but too well" (5.2.340). What different types of love does Othello display, and how is his love significant to the play as a whole? Give examples from the text in your answer.

Q2 How does Shakespeare use structure and language to build tension and contribute to the picture of a society at war?

"I have a weapon / A better never did itself sustain / Upon a soldier's thigh"

Good old Othello, even when it's all gone horribly wrong, he's still up for a bit of double entendre. So what's the lesson we learn from all this? That you need to leave your weapon on the battlefield, instead of taking it to bed. Yep, that sounds about right...

Race

To sum up — Desdemona came first in the egg-and-spoon race, closely followed by Othello. Iago out-sprinted Bianca in the 200 metres, whilst Emilia won the 400 metre hurdles. Brabantio, who came last in every event, won the wooden spoon.

Elizabethan society had Negative Views of Black people

See p.54-55 for more on historical context.

1) Othello is described as a "Moor", but it's not clear what race he is. It's most likely that he was from North Africa, but in Elizabethan times the word 'Moor' could describe anyone with a darker skin tone than a white European.

2) Racial prejudices existed in Elizabethan England. Moors were generally viewed as savages and treated as slaves. This makes Othello an unusual character, because he has risen to prominence in a white society.

3) There was a strong taboo against interracial marriage which is reflected in the play — Othello and Desdemona's marriage is said to be "Against all rules of nature" (1.3.101) and "unnatural" (3.3.231). Interracial marriages were so unlikely that Brabantio actually believes Othello has used "witchcraft" (1.3.64).

4) Many believed that interracial marriage and sex could result in contamination, and some characters in the play suggest that the "lascivious" (1.1.127), black Othello could contaminate the chaste, white Desdemona.

Othello is a Victim of Racism

Elizabeth I complained that there were too many "blackamoors" in England, and twice tried to have them deported.

1) The other characters frequently refer to Othello's race in negative terms:

- Brabantio describes Othello's "sooty bosom" (1.2.70), implying that his colour makes him dirty. He also describes Othello as a "thing" (1.2.71), showing that he doesn't see him as human.

- Iago fuels Brabantio's racist views by presenting him with bestial images of Othello as "a Barbary horse" (1.1.112) and "an old black ram" (1.1.89). This makes Othello seem savage, inhuman and powerful.

- Othello is often referred to using images of hell and the devil because the colour black was linked to evil in Elizabethan times, while the colour white was linked to goodness and innocence. Emilia's comparison of Desdemona and Othello — "the more angel she, / And you the blacker devil!" (5.2.131-132) emphasises this black and white moral divide.

This is linked to the idea that Othello would have been considered to be an 'other' by society (see p.60 for more on this).

2) The only characters who are overtly racist — Iago, Brabantio and Roderigo — are Venetian, and therefore view themselves as 'insiders', at the top of society. Their prejudice may come from a fear of their superior position being undermined by outsiders. This would explain their angry reaction to Othello's success.

3) Iago's persuasive techniques and racist attitudes start to infect Othello's view of himself and he views his race in a negative light. When he suspects Desdemona of infidelity he says "her name [...] is now begrimed and black / As mine own face" (3.3.384-385), which links his race to dirt and acts of evil. This suggests that Othello has internalised the racist attitudes of the other characters — he even worries that Desdemona will discard him because he's black and calls himself a "cursed, cursed slave" (5.2.275).

4) Othello also starts acting in the way that Iago presents him, becoming the racist stereotype that he's told he is — he turns to "savage madness" (4.1.55) and becomes violent when he strikes Desdemona (4.1.240).

Some characters Look Past Othello's Race

1) At the start of the play, Othello uses his race and his 'otherness' as a positive quality. When Brabantio accuses him of 'stealing' Desdemona, he responds eloquently, recognising that his exotic history made Desdemona love him. However, by painting himself as an observer of the "cannibals" (1.3.142), Othello also distances himself from the uncivilised cultures that he describes.

2) Othello is also well-respected in the military — a senator describes him as "valiant" (1.3.47), and the Duke calls him "more fair than black" (1.3.287). However, by suggesting that Othello has the morals of a "fair" or white person he implies that if he was "black", he would be inferior and less virtuous. Even the characters who care for Othello see his race as a bad thing, which needs to be compensated for by his good qualities.

3) Desdemona overlooks Othello's colour, saying that she "saw Othello's visage in his mind" (1.3.249), meaning that his face was transformed because of his "honours and his valiant parts" (1.3.250). Although Desdemona fell in love with Othello's exotic history, she feels a need to defend her decision and his race, which suggests that his race is a weakness.

© Johan Persson / ArenaPAL

Honesty and Deception

This is a page about deception, dictaphones and dinosaurs — honest. It really is. Ok, maybe I'm lying... or am I? I am. I'm not.

Truth *and* Honour *are* Important *in 'Othello'*

'Honest' also meant down-to-earth and unsophisticated. Iago is often described as honest, implying that he's from a lower class — an implication he probably resents.

1) In Shakespeare's time the word '**honest**' had several **meanings** — it was used in the **modern** sense of being **truthful**, but it was also similar in meaning to **honourable**, so it was related to **integrity**. For **women** honesty often meant **chastity**, so women who were **unfaithful** were seen as **dishonest**.

2) The characters use the words "**honest**" and "**honesty**" frequently. **Ironically**, Iago is the character **most often** referred to as honest. This shows how **skilled** he is at **deceiving** others:

- **Cassio** says that he "**never knew a Florentine more kind and honest**" (3.1.39), and **Desdemona** declares "**O, that's an honest fellow**" (3.3.5). This creates an **ironic tension** between the different **meanings** of honesty, because Iago uses his **reputation** for truthfulness to **destroy** Cassio's **honour** and Desdemona's **chastity**.
- **Othello** repeatedly describes Iago as honest — Iago is such a **skilled manipulator** that he persuades Othello that his "**honesty and love doth mince this matter**" (2.3.241) when the **opposite** is true.
- Even **after** he **kills** Desdemona, Othello still calls Iago "**my friend... honest, honest Iago**" (5.2.153).

Deception *and* Self-Deception *are* Common

1) As well as Iago's obvious series of deceptions, **Desdemona** deceives her **father** by marrying Othello, and **Emilia** deceives Desdemona when she **steals** the handkerchief. However, Desdemona and Emilia's deceptive actions are **motivated** by **love**, whereas Iago is **motivated** by **hate** and a **love** of **disorder**.

2) Instead of deceiving others, some characters **deceive themselves**. For example, **Brabantio** believes that his daughter was "**stolen**" (1.3.60) by Othello. He doesn't want to **accept** that Desdemona was "**half the wooer**" (1.3.174).

3) Othello is **blind** to Iago's and Desdemona's **true natures**, and he allows Iago to manipulate him into believing that Desdemona is a "**cunning whore**" (4.2.88) who is "**false as hell**" (4.2.38). Othello's **self-deception** could be seen as just as **important** in bringing about his **downfall** as Iago's deception.

4) Critics such as **F.R. Leavis** agree that Othello is **guilty** of **self-deception** — by the end of the play Othello shows that he doesn't have any **self-knowledge** and **can't deal** with the **situation** (see p.59 for more on this).

'Othello' contains lots of references to sight and blindness. Most tellingly, Othello frequently relies on Iago's eyesight, e.g. "Was not that Cassio parted from my wife?" (3.3.37), just as he trusts Iago's account of events that he hasn't seen.

Appearances *can be* Deceptive

1) Iago makes the other characters **see** what he **wants** them to see. This is shown clearly in Act 4, Scene 1, when he encourages Cassio to talk about **Bianca**, whilst making Othello think that Cassio's remarks are about **Desdemona**.

2) With his **perception warped** by Iago, Othello believes that Desdemona's "**beauty**" (4.1.204) and "**sweet**" smell (4.2.67) **disguise corruption** and **evil**. The **inconsistency** between **appearance** and **reality** in Act 4, Scene 2 shocks Othello. He feels angry that Desdemona appears as **virtuous** as a "**young and rose-lipped cherubin**" when her **alleged betrayal** makes her "**grim as hell**" (lines 62-63).

3) When Othello decides to **kill** Desdemona, he becomes **fixated** on the **whiteness**, the "**monumental alabaster**" (5.2.5), of her skin. To Othello, Desdemona's **appearance undermines** the **link** between white and goodness.

Practice Questions

Q1 'Othello is portrayed as a savage wearing a veneer of western civility.' To what extent do you agree with this statement? Back up your answer with examples from the text.

Q2 'It is self-deception, not deception of others, that drives the characters of *Othello* towards their fate.' To what extent to do you agree with this statement? Refer to the text in your answer.

"I am not what I am"

Is that right, Iago? So you're not really a lying, dastardly egomaniac who's probably planning on world domination once you've sorted out that pesky Othello and the irritating Florentine? It's possible that I may have missed the subtle nuances of the play.

Performing 'Othello'

An Elizabethan performance of 'Othello' would seem strange to a modern audience. Desdemona would have been played by a boy in a dress, and Othello by a white actor. And Iago was played by a fox in a top hat. Um, that last one might not be true.

Shakespeare's plays were **Performed** at the **Globe Theatre**

1) There was an increase in theatre **building** at the end of the **16th century**.

2) **The Lord Chamberlain's Men**, Shakespeare's acting **company**, built the **Globe** in 1599. Archaeologists think that it was a **round**, **three-storey** building with an **open-air** central '**pit**' where the audience could **stand** to watch the plays.

3) More **expensive** seats would be in the **covered** areas around the **outside** of the building, looking down on the **stage** jutting out into the **pit**.

The Globe, rebuilt in 1997, near the site of the original theatre on the bank of the River Thames.

> **The Globe's Reconstruction**
>
> The Globe was burnt down by a misfiring **cannon** during a performance of *Henry VIII* in **1613**. It was **rebuilt**, and then **demolished** again during a **ban** of **theatres** in the **1640s**. A new **Globe Theatre** was rebuilt at the old site in **1997**.

Elizabethan Theatres were **Different** from **Today's Theatres**

1) Shakespeare called the Globe a "**wooden O**" in *Henry V* — it had **round** walls, with the stage **pushed out** into the empty '**pit**' where **spectators** stood. Today's theatres are very different — they **separate** the audience and stage more clearly.

> **Elizabethan Theatre Structure**
>
> • There was **less distinction** between **audience** and **actors** because the **stage** was positioned **among** the **audience**. Instead of an arch, there was a **roof** across the **back half** of the stage, which was **painted** with **clouds** and **stars** to look like the '**heavens**'.
>
> • The stage had no **wings** to **hide props** or **extra characters** and **no curtain** to drop at the **interval** or **scene changes**. Anything that happened **on stage** had to be **part** of the **performance**. Characters that **died** or were **wounded** on stage had to be **carried** off by **other characters**, e.g. after wounding him, **Iago** instructs for **Cassio's body** to be **removed**: "**O, bear him out o'th'air**" (5.1.104).

2) The Elizabethan theatre **wasn't concerned** with looking '**realistic**'. It might seem **odd** to **modern audiences** that all of Shakespeare's plays were performed by a **male-only cast** (as women weren't allowed on stage during Elizabethan times), but the Elizabethan theatre was more about **gesture** and **symbolism** than being '**true**' to life.

'Othello' has a varied **Performance History**

1) *Othello* was first performed in **1604** at court in London. Since then it has been performed at the **Globe**, **Blackfriars Theatre** and at many other theatres around the world for over **400 years**.

2) Throughout its **long performance history**, **actors** have interpreted the character of **Othello** in different ways:

> • **Richard Burbage**, a lead actor in **Shakespeare's theatre company**, was the **first** Othello and his performance is recorded as being **sombre** and **moving**.
>
> • Since Burbage, some actors have adopted a similar style while others have attempted to **explore** Othello's **passionate** and **tempestuous** side. **Tommaso Salvini**, an **Italian actor**, played Othello in the **1880s** and emphasised the **physical violence** in his **interpretation** of the character — his performance **shocked** sensitive 19th-century audiences when he **slapped Desdemona**.

3) Some productions, such as an **1837 production** at **Drury Lane**, London, **alternated** the actors playing **Othello** and **Iago** on a **nightly basis**. This reduces the **differences** between the **two characters** — if the **same actor** plays **both parts**, **questions** are raised about how **similar** the characters are and how much they might have in **common**.

Performing 'Othello'

The play's themes *Challenge Modern Directors*

1) *Othello* is a **popular play** with **modern directors** because it deals with **race** and **gender** issues that are **relevant** today.

2) In **Shakespeare's time**, Othello would have been played by a **white man** — early audiences would have been **shocked** to see a **black actor** on stage, especially one portraying the **marriage** of a **black man** to a **white woman**. The **first black** Othello was played in London, in **1833**, by **Ira Aldridge**, an **African-American actor**. A century later, **Paul Robeson's** celebrated performances in **1930**, **1943** and **1959 familiarised** audiences with a **black actor** playing the **lead role**.

3) However, for most of the **20th century**, many **directors** still **cast** a **white actor** to play the part of "**black Othello**" (2.3.29). This required the actors to wear **black make up** — a procedure called '**blacking up**'. For example, in the **1964** production at the **Royal National Theatre**, the **white actor**, **Laurence Olivier**, '**blacked up**' to play the lead role.

4) Towards the **end** of the **20th century**, and into the **21st**, directors took a more **experimental** approach to **casting** the **roles** to explore the **tensions** between **race** and **gender** in the play:

   - In 1993, a theatre group, **The Acting Initiative**, decided to swap the **genders** of the lead roles, **Othello** and **Desdemona**. The **role reversal** allowed the group to **investigate** Othello's **crime** of **passion** via a **female perspective** and Desdemona's relatively **submissive nature** in the **body** of a **man**.

   - In 1997, the **white** actor **Patrick Stewart** and the director **Jude Kelly** devised an **inverted** production of the play in which a **white Othello** plays opposite an **all-black** cast. This interpretation addressed issues of **racism** by **analysing** how a **white man** might face racism in a **black society**.

   - In 2010, the **Painted Stage company** performed *Othello* as a **three-person**, **all-female cast** to explore the play's **themes** and **relationships** in a different way. The **director, Stewart Melton**, said that the group wanted to reinvent **Desdemona** as "**brave and strong**" for breaking **social taboos**.

Othello's made many *Appearances* on the *Big Screen*

1) *Othello* has been **adapted** for film many times, including **four silent films** made between **1907** and **1922** and various **black** and **white** films. The **1952** film **adaptation** of *Othello*, directed by **Orson Welles**, **focused less** on the **question** of **race**, and instead used the **black and white format** of the **film** to focus on some of the **other themes** of the play, such as Othello's **emotional turmoil**.

2) In **Oliver Parker's** 1995 film, Othello is played by **Laurence Fishburne** — the first **African-American** actor to perform the role **on screen** in a mainstream production. **Kenneth Branagh** plays Iago as a **devious**, **quick-witted character**.

   - Parker's version explores **alternative interpretations** of the play. Some critics argue that **Branagh's portrayal** of Iago implies that he has **homosexual feelings** for Othello.

   - Parker added **new settings** and **actions** to his version, e.g. when Othello demands "**ocular proof**" (3.3.357) from Iago, the **scene** moves to a **beach**, and as Othello becomes increasingly **angry**, he plunges **Iago's head** into the **sea**, giving **force** to his **verbal threat**: "**Make me to see't... or woe upon thy life**" (3.3.361-363).

3) In 2001, Geoffrey Sax's TV film offered a **reinterpretation** of the play in **modern English**. In this version, the setting is **modern-day London** and the film explores **corruption** and **professional jealousy** in the **police force**.

Practice Questions

Q1 How would the Globe's audience's experience of *Othello* be different from that of a cinema-goer in the 20th century?

Q2 What is the significance of Othello's race in the play? Does the effect change if he is played by a white actor?

Q3 If you were directing a modern adaptation of *Othello*, what setting would you use and why?

"I'll see before I doubt"

Try to see at least one performance of 'Othello' before the big ol' eggs-hams. If you can't get hold of a ticket to see it in a theatre, borrow a copy of a film adaptation. It's about the same length as an episode of The X Factor and with just as much weeping.

Form and Structure

'Othello' is a tragedy. And I mean a classical tragedy. Do you follow? No, I don't mean it's just a classic weepie, I mean it's a tragedy according to strict classical principals. Read this page to agree or disagree — 'Othello' doesn't always follow the rules.

Aristotle **Influenced** what people thought about **Tragedies**

1) Tragedy dates back to the **sixth century BC** in **Ancient Greece**. The Greek tragedies have mostly been **lost**, but they were **copied** by the **Roman** playwright, **Seneca**, and Shakespeare was **familiar** with **Seneca's** plays.

2) In the **fourth century BC**, the philosopher **Aristotle** wrote down **rules** for **Greek tragedy** in his *Poetics*:

> A tragedy represents human action.

> The events of the plot are self-contained.

> The events are serious, and the characters have a high social status.

Aristotle said that:

"**Tragedy is an imitation of an action** that is admirable, **complete**, and possesses **magnitude**; in language made pleasurable, each of its species separated in different parts; in the form of **action, not through narration**; effecting **through pity and fear the purification of such emotions.**"

> It's acted rather than simply being described.

> Tragedy creates pity and fear in the audience, but the ending purges them of these feelings. This 'purging' is called catharsis.

3) Aristotle said that tragedy should focus on a **noble character** who makes a **mistake**. This leads to their **downfall** as the **hero** is **punished** severely. In the end, however, the noble hero **gains** some **self-knowledge** and, partially at least, **redeems** their reputation.

Othello is a noble character

Othello's **mistake** (giving in to **jealousy**) has **terrible consequences** and leads to his **downfall**. At the end he **realises** that he is "**one, not easily jealous but, being wrought, / Perplexed in the extreme**" (5.2.341-342).

4) Aristotle said that tragedies should have **unity** of **action** — **every event** should **contribute** to the **plot**. Neoclassicists expanded this idea, and said that tragedies should also have **unity** of **time** and **place**. They thought a 'perfect' tragedy should take place in **one location** over **one day** and all actions should be **directly relevant** to the plot.

Othello, the play, does not follow these unities

The action starts in **Venice** but moves to Cyprus. The **events** seem to unfold quite **quickly** but over an **uncertain period** of time — the **time span** could be days or weeks (see p.47).

Othello shares similarities with **Domestic Tragedy**

1) The play opens as if it will be a **political tragedy** — the **Turks** are set to invade **Cyprus** and it's **Othello's** role to hold back the **invasion**.

2) However, the **political situation** becomes just a **backdrop** to the **personal tragedy** that unfolds. The action increasingly focuses on a **small number** of **characters** and their **relationships** with each other.

3) This links to '**domestic tragedy**', a **dramatic genre** in the **late 16th century** which focused on the lives of the **middle** and **lower classes**. Although *Othello* is about mostly **upper-class characters**, Shakespeare focuses on their private lives in a more **domestic setting**.

4) The **themes** in *Othello* are **personal ones** — jealousy, love, deception and revenge. The play **explores** the **inner workings** of the **human mind** more closely than issues of **war** and **political conflict**.

© Johan Persson / ArenaPAL

Death in Domestic Spaces

- In **Greek tragedy**, **domestic** space was **clearly separated** from **public**. **Dramatic conventions** dictated where characters should **die**, e.g. a **hero** should die on **stage**, while a **woman** should die **inside** the **house**, off stage.

- Othello's **murder** of **Desdemona** takes place in the most **intimate domestic space** — their **bedroom**. However, the **bedroom** is in **full view** of the **audience**, and is soon filled with **officials**. This shows that the **political** and the **private** have become **confused** and the **intimacy** of Othello and Desdemona's marriage has been **violated**.

Form and Structure

Othello has *Two Settings* — *Venice* and *Cyprus*

1) Act 1 is set in **Venice** but from Act 2 the play is set in **Cyprus**. The two locations are very **different**:

Venice	Cyprus
• **Venice** was seen as a **civilised, lawful place**. It's associated with **power, commerce** and **wealth**. • **Venetian society** had a **liberal attitude** towards **sex** — **Venetian women** were thought to be **promiscuous**.	• **Cyprus** is **isolated**. The **island** has **associations** with **hostility** and **conflict** — Cassio calls Cyprus **"this warlike isle"** (2.1.43). Even after the **Turkish Fleet** have been **defeated**, there are lots of '**conflicts**' on the **island**. • The move from '**civilised**', Christian **Venice** to **warlike, wild Cyprus** removes the characters from their **normal environment**, creating **disorder** and **isolation**.

2) **Initially**, we get some sense that **Shakespeare** is creating a **wider world** than the one of the **main characters**:

- In Act 1, the **Turkish fleet** is aiming to attack Cyprus when they suddenly take a **detour**, and head for **Rhodes** — for a **brief time**, the **Turks' voyage** looks like it might map out a **larger territory**.
- However, at the **beginning** of Act 2 the **Turkish fleet** is **destroyed** by a storm. The **storm foreshadows** the **destructive passions** that will **cause problems** on the **island**. With the **external** threat of war **removed**, the setting in Cyprus becomes **claustrophobic** as the focus increasingly closes in on just **one couple** — Othello and Desdemona.

The *Passage* of *Time* in the play is *Unclear*

1) When **Shakespeare** adapted the plot of *Othello* from his **source material** (see p.54), he compressed the **time frame** into a few days. This makes the **passage** of time **ambiguous** — it seems like **Othello's marriage** and his **growing jealousy** happen **quickly**, but the characters **say things** that **imply** time is moving more **slowly**.

2) **Critics**, such as A.C. Bradley, **consider** that there are **two possible accounts** of the length of **time** the play covers:

A Short Time Frame	A Long Time Frame
This suggests that the play spans just **three days**: **Day 1** — Venice **Day 2** — Arrival in Cyprus **Day 3** — The start of Act 3, Scene 3 to the end. This time frame is **intense** and would mean that Desdemona is **murdered** within a **few days** of arriving in Cyprus. This means that Iago manages to **drive** Othello to **murderous jealousy** very **quickly**.	The play seems to cover a **longer period of time**: **Bianca complains** to Cassio that he has **stayed away** from her for a **week**, "**What! Keep a week away? Seven days and nights?**" (3.4.169). This would mean that Desdemona is **murdered** within a **few weeks** of arriving in Cyprus which makes the **action seem more realistic**.

3) Shakespeare seems to use the **two** time frames **alongside** one another. The **longer time scale** makes Othello's **change** in **character** more **plausible** whilst the **shorter time scale** provides **dramatic intensity**.

Practice Questions

Q1 How does Othello, as a character, arouse both 'pity' and 'fear' in the audience?

Q2 What is the relationship between the private and the political in *Othello*? Can they easily be separated?

Q3 How does Shakespeare use time and setting to emphasise Othello's emotional breakdown?

"Torments will ope your lips"

Tragedy's been around for thousands of years and still no one quite knows what it is, but I reckon I've nailed it — there should be unity of time, space and... Oh, not always? Ok, but there should be a baddy. Sometimes the baddy is also a goody? What is this?

Dramatic Language

"Suddenly, there was the silhouette of a tall and menacing figure" — wait, this isn't what we mean by 'dramatic language'. No. Shakespeare didn't start every line with "OMG!" and end every scene with a car chase. Well, sometimes he came close...

Shakespeare uses *Blank Verse* to imitate the rhythm of *Natural Speech*

© Nigel Norrington / ArenaPAL

1) The **rhythm** of English speech **naturally** follows a **pattern** of emphasising **every other syllable**.

2) This rhythm is called **iambic**. An **iamb** is a **measurement** of **two syllables** that goes 'duh-**dum**'. A string of **five iambs** makes **ten syllables** of alternating stress — this is called **iambic pentameter**:

> 1 2 3 4 5 6 7 8 9 10
> "The **robbed** that **smiles** steals **some**thing **from** the **thief**" (1.3.206)
> (duh - **dum**) (duh - **dum**) (duh - **dum**) (duh - **dum**) (duh - **dum**)

3) In the sixteenth century, poets started to write in **unrhymed** iambic pentameter — this is called **blank verse**.

4) Shakespeare uses the **10-syllable framework** of **blank verse** to imitate **formal** speech — lines that are written in **blank verse** are usually spoken by **high-status** characters (e.g. Othello or the Duke) or form part of a **speech** or **soliloquy**.

5) At some points the **steady rhythm** of blank verse is **interrupted** by a **caesura** (break). E.g. In Act 5, Scene 2, Othello's speech is broken by an **emotional pause**. The pause adds extra **weight** to the word "**fatal**" and makes the final three words of the line seem **heavy** and **slow**.

> ⟁caesura⟁
>
> 1 2 3 4 5 6 7 ↓ 8 9 10
> So **sweet** was so **ne'er** so **fa**tal. **I** must **weep**. (5.2.20)
> (duh - **dum**) (duh - **dum**) (duh-**dum**)(duh - **dum**) (duh - **dum**)

Sometimes the verse *Breaks Down* into *Prose*

1) Prose is writing that's **not verse** — it **doesn't rhyme**, it's got **no metre** and there are **no line breaks**.

2) When characters **talk** to each other **informally** or address a character of a **lower social status**, they use **prose**.

3) At other points, the characters' **control** over their **language slips**, which reflects their state of **mind**. Prose can be used to show that a character can't **organise** their **thoughts** in **eloquent iambic pentameter**.

> In Act 4, Scene 1 Othello's speech **switches** from **iambic pentameter** to **prose** as he is so **distressed** by the idea that Desdemona had **sex** with Cassio. The **breakdown** of his **speech** mirrors an **emotional breakdown** as Othello "*falls*" into a **trance** after shouting in prose: "**Is't possible? Confess! Handkerchief! O devil!**" (4.1.42-43)

Shakespeare uses *Rhetoric* to give his *Language* more *Power*

1) Shakespeare's language is full of **tricks** and **flourishes** that make his writing more **powerful**. These **techniques** are part of a **general practice** of making **speeches persuasive** called '**rhetoric**'.

2) Shakespeare often uses these **rhetorical devices** (see glossary for more):

Repetition	**Alliteration** (placing words that begin with the same sound near each other) and **anaphora** (starting phrases or sentences with the same word).	"Not to pick **b**ad from **b**ad, but **b**y **b**ad mend!" (4.3.104)
Puns	**Homophones** are different words that sound the same and **homographs** are words that have the same spelling.	The word '**lie**', which means to be dishonest and to lie down, also had sexual connotations in Shakespeare's time: "**Lie with** her? **lie on** her? We say **lie on** her when they **belie** her!" (4.1.35-36)
Exaggeration	Use of **hyperbole** (stretching the point for emphasis) and **superlatives** (saying something is the "most" or "least").	"**Most** fortunately: he hath achieved a maid / That **paragons description** and **wild fame**" (2.1.61-62)

Dramatic Language

Characters **Speak** their **Minds** in **Soliloquies**

1) In *Othello*, characters sometimes **express** their **thoughts** to each other but often just to **themselves**.

- **Short outbursts** or **comments** directed at the **audience** are called **asides**, e.g. when Othello sees Bianca with his handkerchief, he says to the audience: **"By heaven, that should be my handkerchief!"** (4.1.157-158) as confirmation of his **suspicions**.
- A **long speech** delivered to **other characters** on stage is called a **monologue**, e.g. In Act 1, Scene 3 Othello explains to the Duke how his **relationship** with **Desdemona** developed. After being invited to speak, **"Say it, Othello"**(1.3.126), he speaks for 42 lines **without interruption**.
- A **long speech** performed in **private**, or while the character **thinks** they are **alone**, is called a **soliloquy**. Soliloquies are **introspective reflections** that **communicate** the character's **inner thoughts** to the **audience**, e.g. when **Othello** is left alone in Act 3, Scene 3, he tells the audience that he does **genuinely** trust Iago, calling him a man of **"exceeding honesty"** (3.3.255).

2) Even when Iago is **speaking alone**, he never makes it **clear** whether he is **trusting** the **audience** with **secrets** or **tricking** them with **lies** — this makes the audience **doubt** the reliability of Iago's soliloquies.

The characters' **Personalities** are **Expressed** in their **Language**

1) Othello's **language** is **grand** and **dignified**, reflecting his **status** as a **military hero**. He claims his **speech** is too **"rude"** (**basic**) for the **"soft phrase of peace"** (1.3.81-82) because he's used to the **rough language** of **battle**.

2) However, Othello's speech is just as **powerful** away from the **battlefield**. He redirects his **passion** into **poetic declarations** of **love**. Desdemona falls in **love** with Othello because of the **stories** he tells her — Othello says that Desdemona would **"Devour up my discourse"** (1.3.149) because **"She loved me for the dangers I had passed"** (1.3.166).

3) In contrast, **Iago's speech** is **varied** and he changes his **language** to take **advantage** of each **situation**:

- Iago **flatters** Roderigo: **"Why, now I see there's mettle in thee, and even from this instant do I build on thee a better opinion than ever before"** (4.2.204-205). His **flattery** wins **Roderigo's trust** and **fidelity** so **Iago** can then **use** him against Cassio.
- Iago uses **crude sexual innuendo** to **indirectly remind** Othello of Desdemona's supposed **infidelity** — he **surrounds** Othello with **base language** that **influences** his **thoughts** and **decisions**: **"Were they as prime as goats, as hot as monkeys"** (3.3.400).

4) As **Iago's influence** over Othello increases, he starts to affect **Othello's choice** of **words**:

- After **Emilia** insists **Desdemona** is **honest**, Othello reacts as Iago would have done — he **condemns** Emilia as a **"simple bawd"** and seems to be troubled by the **idea** that his **wife** is **"a subtle whore"** (4.2.19-20). This **contrasts sharply** with the **thoughtful** and **poised** Othello of the earlier scenes.
- Othello's language becomes preoccupied with **hell** and **damnation**. He shouts **"Fire and brimstone!"** (4.1.232) and **strikes Desdemona** as he calls her **"Devil!"** (4.1.240). This is very **similar** to Iago's **language** in Act 1, Scene 3: **"Hell and night / Must bring this monstrous birth to the world's light"** (1.3.397-398).

Practice Questions

Q1 "I think this tale would win my daughter too." (1.3.170).
Read Act 1, Scene 3, from lines 126 to 170. Analyse the role of blank verse and rhetoric in Othello's persuasive speech.

Q2 Discuss the importance of asides and soliloquies in relation to the play's audience.

Q3 In Act 3, Scene 3 Iago has approximately fifty percent more lines than Othello. Is it the volume or skill of Iago's speech that persuades Othello to doubt his wife?

"This is the only witchcraft that I have used"

Okay, okay, so Othello tries some natty tricks with his verbal "witchcraft" and seduces Desdemona. But he meets his match with Iago — this talk of "witchcraft" only foreshadows Othello's own seduction under the 'spell' of Iago's persuasive powers.

Dramatic Language

There are seven soliloquies in 'Othello'. They're tricky things to get your head around and Shakespeare's thrown his best at them — they're dense and poetic. So to give you a head start here are four extracts with some examples of close reading.

"That Cassio loves her, I do well believ't" (2.1.277-303)

The **audience** don't know if Iago is telling the **truth**. He calls Othello "**the lusty Moor**" (1.2.286) and claims Othello has slept with Emilia, but only a few lines earlier he describes Othello as a "**most dear husband**" (2.1.282) — even in his **soliloquies** he's **deceptive** and **inconsistent**. This duplicity seems to **expose** Iago as a **victim** of his own **paranoid** thoughts — he fears Othello and Cassio "**with my night-cap too**" (2.1.298), worried that everyone is **cuckolding** him. But as he **begins** and **ends** his **soliloquy** with a **rhyming couplet**, he signals that his **speech** is more of a **controlled performance**, full of **plans for action** rather than **insecure worries**.

Caesura

Punctuation breaks up the **iambic pentameter**, forcing a **caesura** just after Iago reveals his plans to make Othello jealous. This allows the **moment** to **expand** into a **dramatic pause**.

And nothing can or shall content my soul
Till I am evened with him, wife for wife.
Or, failing so, yet that I put the Moor
At least into a jealousy so strong
That judgement cannot cure. Which thing to do,
If this poor trash of Venice, whom I leash
For his quick hunting, stand the putting on,
I'll have our Michael Cassio on the hip
                                    (289-296)

Pun

"**Wife for wife**" is an **adaption** of the **Biblical law** "**life for life**" (Exodus 21:23). Iago seems to be seeking **justification** for '**revenge**' by **echoing scripture** and referring to "**my soul**". Iago later says he'd instead settle for making **Othello** mad with **jealousy** — his **aims change** which suggests he lacks **real motives** for **revenge**.

Metaphor

Iago uses a **series** of **hunting metaphors**. "**Trash**" was a verb meaning 'to **restrain hounds**' while **hunting** and a "**leash**" is used to **restrain** dogs. Also, "**on the hip**" was a **wrestling** term. Iago's **language** is **aggressive** and **predatory**.

"And what's he then that says I play the villain?" (2.3.326-352)

This **soliloquy** comes at the **end** of a **scene** in which Iago **manipulates** those around him. He has **convinced** Cassio to **drink**, **persuaded** Othello to **suspend Cassio** and **told Cassio** to ask **Desdemona** for help. In his **soliloquy** he unveils his **reasons** — and his plan to "**enmesh**" everyone in a "**net**" made from their own **goodness**.

Rhetorical Question

In his soliloquy, Iago shows his **defensive nature** by using rhetorical questions to suggest that people might **suspect** he's a **villain** — once in the **opening line** and again at the **midpoint** of the soliloquy. It seems that Iago is anticipating **criticism** and **rumour** — **two strong forces** which he plans to use himself, describing them as "**pestilence**" (2.3.346), i.e. a **disease** that can **infect trust** and **relationships**.

Alliteration

The repeated 'c', 'd' and 'p' sounds link lines into small groups as Iago announces the stages of his plan. The harsh 'c' sounds match the affronted tone of his question which leads to the repeated 'p' sounds as his plans start to take shape.

How am I then a villain

To counsel Cassio to this parallel course,
Directly to his good? Divinity of hell!
When devils will the blackest sins put on,
They do suggest at first with heavenly shows,
As I do now: for whiles this honest fool
Plies Desdemona to repair his fortunes
And she for him pleads strongly to the Moor,
I'll pour this pestilence into his ear
                                    (338-346)

Paradox

The idea of a '**divinity**' of '**hell**' is a **paradox** that summarises Iago's **evil logic**. There is **no god in hell** but this phrase makes sense if Iago is referring to **himself** as a **devil**, with a "**heavenly**" **appearance** and **evil intentions**. **Paradoxes** link to the "**parallel course**" that Iago imagines taking Cassio on — a path that will lead to **evil** while **appearing** to **help** Cassio.

Dramatic Language

"This fellows of exceeding honesty" (3.3.255-274)

Othello's **soliloquy** is at the **turning** point of the **longest scene** in the play. In this **intense** scene, Iago is able to exert his **influence** on Othello **without interruption**. Othello's **soliloquy** is the **only moment** he's **alone**, and it shows that he is **uncertain** of Iago's claims. However, Iago's verbal **assault** successfully **alters** Othello's **attitude** towards his "**sweet Desdemon**" (3.3.55) by the end of the scene.

Metaphor

Othello uses an **extended metaphor** in which he is a **falconer** and Desdemona an **untamed hawk** ("**haggard**"). In place of **falconer's straps** ("**jesses**") Othello imagines his own "**heart strings**".

This fellow's of exceeding honesty,
And knows all qualities with a learnèd spirit,
Of human dealings. If I do prove her haggard,
Though that her jesses were my dear heart-strings,
I'd whistle her off, and let her down the wind
To prey at fortune. Haply, for I am black
And have not those soft parts of conversation

(255-61)

Blank Verse

This is the **second** time Othello claims to be "**rude**" (1.3.81) in speech. Earlier the claim was **false modesty**. Now, however, Othello's **confidence** is **low** — he lists his **race** and his **education** as flaws.

Pun

'Prey' is a **homophone** of 'pray'. **Metaphorically**, Desdemona must hunt the 'prey' that **fortune provides** (she must make her **own way**). As part of the **pun**, Desdemona must '**pray**' for **good fortune**, because she has **sinned**.

"It is the cause, it is the cause, my soul" (5.2.1-22)

If you're not sure what any of these words mean check the glossary on p.70-71.

Othello's lines are full of **repeated phrases** and **sounds** — the **structure** of his speech suggests that he is trying to set his **resolve** to **kill** his wife by **repeating** his **intentions** aloud.

Anaphora

The **same phrase** is **repeated within** these lines. This **repetition** allows Othello to **sound certain** of the **existence** of his "**cause**" while remaining **vague** about what the "**cause**" is. He addresses "**my soul**" as if he is trying to **convince himself**.

It is the cause, it is the cause, my soul:
Let me not name it to you, you chaste stars!
It is the cause. Yet I'll not shed her blood,
Nor scar that whiter skin of hers than snow,
And smooth as monumental alabaster:
Yet she must die, else she'll betray more men.
Put out the light, and then put out the light

(1-7)

Sibilance

This passage is full of **sibilant sounds** (repeated 's' sounds) — **whispering** 'sh', 'sc' and 'sk' and **softer** sounds of 'sn' and 'sm'. The **soft 's'** creates a **calming** effect, like a **lullaby**. This **contrasts** with the **terrible** act **Othello** is about to **commit**.

Figurative Language

This repetition emphasises that 'light' can refer to both **literal** and **figurative** lights — the actual **candle light** and the **symbolic** '**light**' of Desdemona's **life**.

Practice Questions

Q1 Reread Iago's soliloquy in Act 2, Scene 1, lines 277 to 303. Do you think Iago is convinced of his wife's affairs or is he just looking for excuses to launch his attacks on Othello, Cassio and Roderigo?

Q2 How do Othello's soliloquies influence the audience's understanding of his rapid change to jealousy?

Q3 Discuss Othello's use of rhetorical devices in his soliloquies and how this changes over the course of the play.

"And out of her own goodness make the net / That shall enmesh them all."

Wowsers. Iago's certainly got a way with words to convince Othello so quickly. But then, looking at Othello's soliloquies, it's possible to argue that he was a suggestible kind of guy, with half-buried self-esteem issues just waiting to be dug up again. Whoops.

Irony and Double Meanings

Shakespeare has given you a big box full of snazzy tricks so you can amaze your friends. And when I say 'box', I mean 'play'. And when I say 'snazzy tricks', I mean 'linguistic techniques'. 'Amaze'? Yes, I mean 'struggle with'. 'Friends'? Ok, 'revision'.

Situational Irony reverses Expectations in the Action

Irony is a technique that takes advantage of the difference between what is said and what is meant, or what is supposed to happen and what actually happens.

© Johan Persson / ArenaPAL

> ### Situational Irony
> Situational irony is where **events** turn out to have the **opposite result** of what was originally **intended**.

1) In **tragedy**, **situational irony heightens** the sense of **misfortune**, as **events** seem to **conspire** against the **characters**:

> Often the **tragic ending's proximity** to a **happy outcome** makes the **loss harder** to **bear**, e.g. Desdemona is **murdered** by her **husband** on their **marital bed**, a **location** associated with **love** and **intimacy**.

2) **Situational irony** is a **contradiction** of a **character's expectations**. Unlike other types of **irony**, it doesn't appeal to the audience's **awareness** that the play is a **work** of **fiction** — a character can also be aware of **situational irony**.

3) The **sense** of **irony** is **found** in how the end result relates to the intended, e.g. **Iago** hopes to **destroy Cassio's reputation**, but by the **end of the play** it is actually **Iago's own reputation** that has been destroyed.

Dramatic Irony appeals to the Audience's Awareness of the Performance

> ### Dramatic Irony
> Dramatic irony occurs when the **audience** has **knowledge** of something that the **characters** on stage **don't**.

1) Dramatic irony is created by the audience's **double perspective** of the play. The audience are aware of their **own position** watching the action on stage and the **characters'** own viewpoints.

2) This **double perspective** encourages the **audience** to explore the **relationship** between **appearance** and **reality**, **truth** and **deception**. **Dramatic irony** helps to build up **tension** as the tragic ending seems **inevitable**.

3) The way that the **audience** see the handkerchief being **exchanged** is an example of **dramatic irony**:

> The audience see the **handkerchief** fall in Act 3, Scene 3, line 285 and be **picked up** by **Emilia** three lines later. **Iago** then **discloses** his **plans** for this handkerchief: "**I will in Cassio's lodging lose this napkin, / And let him find it**" (3.3.318-319). The **audience** is aware of Iago's **plans** to use the **handkerchief** to arouse Othello's **jealousy** as well as the **innocent** way the **handkerchief** was **dropped**. This **increases** the **tension** as the audience watch Othello **accuse** his **wife** of **offering** it to Cassio.

Verbal Irony helps to establish Iago's Character

> ### Verbal Irony
> Verbal irony occurs when a **character says something** that is actually the **opposite** of the **truth**.

1) Unlike **dramatic** or **situational** irony, **verbal irony** can be used **intentionally** by the character themselves.

2) In *Othello*, the **audience know** Iago's **intentions** (**dramatic irony**) mean that his **speech** is full of **verbal irony**.

> ### Iago's Duplicity creates Verbal Irony
> - Iago describes himself as being as "**honest as I am**" (2.1.195) and declares that "**Men should be what they seem**" (3.3.125). This is an **instance** of **verbal irony** as Iago knows himself to be **dishonest** and has **previously** told **Roderigo** that he is only "**seeming so for my particular end**" (1.1.61) — his announcement "**I am not what I am**" (1.1.66) directly **contradicts** his **advice** in Act 3.
> - However, when he says to Othello, "**My lord, you know I love you**" (3.3.116) and "**what is spoke comes from my love**" (3.3.214-215), it's likely that these lines are **ironic**. However, the **audience can't be sure** whether Iago is being **honest** or **dishonest** — many critics have **wondered** whether Iago has **homosexual feelings** for Othello (see p.27).

Irony and Double Meanings

Shakespeare uses *Double Meanings* to add *Ambiguity* to his *Language*

1) Shakespeare uses **words** that carry **multiple meanings**, using both **ambiguous wordplay** and **bawdy innuendo**. This allows **characters** like **Iago** to create **disorder** through **language**.

2) Shakespeare gives Iago many lines of **sexual innuendo** to reflect the **character's moral depravity** and **quick wit**.

> Iago tells Brabantio that **"your daughter and the Moor are making the beast with two backs"** (1.1.116-118), using a **euphemism** to suggest the **image** of Othello and Desdemona having **sex**.

3) Iago picks out the **double meanings** in the **other characters'** speech, causing them to **question themselves**.

> When Othello says that **Cassio "went between us very oft"** (3.3.99) he means that Cassio acted as a **messenger** between **Othello** and **Desdemona** during their courtship. Iago's response is an **exclamation, "Indeed!"** (3.3.100), that **provocatively** suggests that Othello should be **suspicious** of this, and perhaps even that **Cassio** was **"between"** Othello and Desdemona **physically**.

Oxymorons and *Paradoxes* keep *Opposites Close Together*

1) *Othello* is a play of **opposites**. The colours **black** and **white** are used to convey **contrasting symbolic** ideas — **black** is **conventionally associated** with **evil**, **sin** and **hell**, while **white** is linked to **goodness**, **purity** and **innocence**.

2) However, Shakespeare **resists** the simple **opposition** of **black** and **white**:

- **Bianca** means 'white'. The fact she is a **prostitute** undermines **usual associations** of white with 'purity'.
- **Othello**, the **"black ram"** (1.1.89) **embodies** the opposition of **good** and **evil** in the play. The **distinction** between **black** and **white** is blurred further when the **Duke** tells Brabantio that Othello is **"far more fair than black"** (1.3.287) — the word 'fair' was a **synonym** for 'light-coloured' and 'honest'. The word's **double meaning** introduces the **idea** that Othello doesn't **fit** in with the **characters'** racial **stereotypes**.

3) This **breakdown** of **clear oppositions** means that the play is full of **oxymorons**:

> **Oxymoron**
> An **oxymoron** is when **two words** which **contradict** each other are placed **together**.

4) Othello refers to Desdemona as **"the fair devil"** (3.3.475). The use of the word 'fair', meaning '**honest**', shows Othello's **confused attitude** towards Desdemona — he sees her as **beautiful** but **deceitful** and repeatedly refers to her in contradictory terms: **"O thou weed / Who art so lovely fair"** (4.2.66-67).

5) As 'fair' also means 'pale', **"fair devil"** is also an **oxymoron**, as **unholiness** was associated with **blackness**. This **oxymoron** echoes **Iago's** earlier **line** when he explains that some **"devils"** use **angelic** **"heavenly shows"** to **hide** their **"blackest sins"** (2.3.341-342).

6) The **opposition** of **ideas** in *Othello* results in characters **contradicting** themselves:

> **Paradox**
> A **paradox** is the result of an **apparently true** statement which seems to **contradict** itself.

When Iago says **"I am not what I am"** (1.1.66) the sentence is a **paradox** which expresses the **idea** that he is **not** what he **appears**. When Iago says, **"In following him, I follow but myself"** (1.1.59) it seems paradoxical, but what he means is he will appear to be **supportive** of **Othello**, while working for his own **ends**.

Practice Questions

Q1 How does Shakespeare use dramatic irony in Act 3, Scene 3 to build suspense before Othello's tragic downfall?

Q2 What is the role of sexual innuendo in Iago's speech? What does it tell the audience about Iago's character?

Q3 Read Act 4, Scene 2, lines 69-80. The word 'committed' (meaning 'done something') was an Elizabethan euphemism for 'commit adultery'. How does the word's double meaning affect Othello's reaction to his wife's question?

"I think my wife is honest, and think she is not"

It's ironic that it's actually Desdemona's concern for Othello and his own bleedin' impatience that lets the handkerchief fall. If he hadn't pushed her away maybe the whole play would have ended with hugs and kisses. How ironic. Which kind of irony, though?

Cultural Context

Cultural context is suspiciously like a history lesson. Sorry, but it'll help you understand what Shakespeare was thinking when he wrote 'Othello'. At the time it was about as controversial as a chocolate fruit pizza — a genuinely strange dish...

Shakespeare was Writing in a Renaissance

1) The Renaissance was a **cultural movement** inspired by the **Classical arts** that took place in Europe between the **14th** and **17th century**. It was an artistic and intellectual '**rebirth**' which **challenged old traditions**. It **began** in **Italy**, and centred on **Florence** and **Siena**. Florence became known as a **cultural centre**, which embraced **Renaissance ideas** and was **home** to **famous scholars** such as **Niccolò Machiavelli** (see p.67).

2) The Renaissance celebrated **reason** and **improving mankind's abilities** as far as possible. This gave birth to the idea of a '**Renaissance man**' — a 'Renaissance man' was expected to be **well-rounded** with **knowledge** of all of the **arts**. They were expected to be **brave**, **intelligent** and **well-spoken**.

3) Shakespeare was **influenced** by the **Renaissance** when he wrote *Othello*:

- It encouraged **Shakespeare** to **challenge traditional values** — he portrayed Othello, an **ethnic minority**, as a **noble** and **civilised hero**, whilst making Iago, a **white man**, **immoral** and **destructive**.
- The **importance** of **reason** is **emphasised** — Othello tries to **maintain** his "**best judgment**" (2.3.200) and wants "**proof**" (3.3.383) of Desdemona's **betrayal**. **Emotions** are **portrayed** as extreme and **destructive** in the play.

'Othello' was Written at a time when Theatre was Changing

1) **Before** the Renaissance, there were **no theatre companies**, plays were quite **short** and were usually **religious**.

2) **Morality plays** were **popular** — these were **allegorical plays** where sins and virtues were **personified**. These plays focused on a **man** who **gives in** to **temptation** and then **repents**. Shakespeare would have been **influenced** by this **tradition**.

The character of Iago may have been based on the type of 'Vice' characters that were seen in morality plays.

3) The Renaissance **encouraged dramatists** to focus on **Classical drama** — they started to take **old texts** and **rework** them. People who went to see plays **expected** to know the **plot** but hoped to see a **skilled playwright** introduce **new elements** to the story.

4) As a result, plays got **longer** and were **inspired** by **history** and **legend**. Shakespeare took his **inspiration** for *Othello* from an **Italian short story** called *Un Capitano Moro* ('A Moorish Captain'). *Un Capitano Moro* was written by **Cinthio**, an **Italian novelist** and **poet**, and was **first published** in 1565.

Shakespeare Adapted the Original Story

In Cinthio, the handkerchief was also important in proving Desdemona's guilt.

Shakespeare's play is clearly **inspired** by **Cinthio's story** — most of the **characters** and the basic **plot** are similar. In Cinthio's story 'The Moor' **marries Disdemona**, and is **persuaded** by 'The Ensign' that she's having an **affair** with 'The Captain'. Shakespeare introduced some **key differences**:

1) Shakespeare **added new characters** such as Roderigo, and gave Cinthio's characters names — '**The Moor**' became Othello, '**The Ensign**', Iago, and '**The Captain**', Cassio. He also made his characters more rounded, giving **minor characters** like **Bianca** a more **important role**.

2) The ending is **significantly different** — in Cinthio's story 'The Ensign' and 'The Moor' **murder** Disdemona together, and collapse the ceiling to make it look like an accident.

3) The **setting** is the same — both stories begin in **Venice**, before the action moves to **Cyprus**. However, the **backdrop** of the **Cyprus conflict** was added by Shakespeare.

4) Shakespeare dramatically **changed** the **time frame** that the events take place in — he suggests **two possible time frames**, and **sped up** the play's **climax** (see p.47).

5) Shakespeare also **developed Iago's motives** — in Cinthio's story 'The Ensign' is clearly **motivated** by **lust** for Disdemona, but Shakespeare added other **potential motivations** such as a hatred of Othello and sexual jealousy of Cassio. He also made Iago's **true motive** more **ambiguous**, which makes Iago seem more like a **motiveless force** of **evil**.

6) The **moral** of Cinthio's story is that **European women** shouldn't **marry outside** of their **race**. The **moral** of Shakespeare's play (if there is one) is much more **ambiguous**, leaving the audience to draw their **own conclusions**.

Cultural Context

'Othello' was Influenced by the Cyprus Conflict

Shakespeare probably used 'The History of the Turks' by Richard Knolles for information on the Cyprus conflict.

1) Cyprus was a **highly prized island** because of its **natural resources** and **military significance** — it was **located** in the **middle** of the **Turkish Empire**, so would have been **useful** for **attacking** the Turks.

2) When Shakespeare was writing, **Italy** was divided into **separate states** under **different rulers**. **Venice** was one of the **wealthiest sovereign states**. It engaged in **war** for **profit** and **hired mercenaries** (**paid foreign soldiers**) like Cassio and Othello, to **fight** in the **army**.

3) In 1489, Venice **took control** of Cyprus, but by 1571 the Turks had **captured it**. Shakespeare was **writing** *Othello* in 1603, at a time when the **Turks ruled Cyprus**, which would have given the play a **heavy irony** because the Venetians' **victory** was to be **short-lived**.

4) Even though *Othello* was **written** at a **time** when the **Venetians** (and the **English**) had a **peaceful relationship** with the Turks, the Turks were still **perceived negatively** in Western Europe:

- The phrase **'to turn Turk'** was **commonly used**, and is seen in *Othello*: "**Are we turned Turks?**" (2.3.164). This originally meant **'to convert to Islam'** but it had taken on **other meanings** — it also meant **'to change for the worse'**, **'to become a traitor'** and it could mean **'to commit adultery'** or **'to become a whore'**.

- Both Iago and Othello 'turn Turk' — Iago's a **traitor** and Othello **changes** for the **worse**. In **Act 5, Scene 2** Othello **implies** that **both men** are **like** a "**turbaned Turk**" (5.2.349) that he once **killed**.

The play Reflects the Social Concerns of the Time

STEREOTYPES

1) Racial stereotypes in **Elizabethan England** presented **Moors** as **violent savages**. This can be seen in the **literature** of the time, where they were portrayed as **lustful, dangerous villains** (e.g. Aaron in *Titus Andronicus*).

2) At the beginning of the play Othello is **noble** and **self-controlled**, which goes **against** these stereotypes, though Othello's **savagery** at the play's **end** could be seen to confirm them. Iago also calls Othello a "**barbarian**" (1.3.351), Roderigo calls him "**thick-lips**" (1.1.67) and Brabantio calls him a "**thing**" (1.2.71).

3) **Venetians** were thought to be **sophisticated**, but **Venetian women** were seen as **promiscuous** — Iago **voices** these **stereotypes** when he calls Desdemona a "**super-subtle Venetian**" (1.3.351), and implies that Venetian women are **unfaithful** — "**In Venice they do let God see the pranks / They dare not show their husbands**" (3.3.200-201).

4) **Florentines** were seen as **educated**, because Florence was the **birthplace** of the **Renaissance** and Cassio seems to follow this **stereotype** — Iago calls him a "**great arithmetician**" and the "**bookish theoric**" (1.1.19 and 24).

GENDER ROLES

1) **Women** were **financially dependent** on first their **father** and then their **husband** when they **married**. They had **few rights** and were seen as **less intelligent** than men. Shakespeare's **audience** would have **sympathised** with Brabantio's **reaction** to Desdemona's marriage because he was **responsible** for finding her an **appropriate husband**.

2) **Women** were expected to be **virgins** until **marriage**, and a **man's honour** was **closely tied** to his **wife's** (and **daughter's**) reputation. This is why Othello is so **distraught** about the idea of Desdemona's **infidelity**.

3) **Interracial marriages** were seen as "**nature, erring from itself**" (3.3.226), **scandalous** and **unusual** in Elizabethan England. Desdemona's marriage **challenges Brabantio's authority** and **social convention**, especially because she played an **active part** in their **courtship**.

4) However, Desdemona is also **traditional** because she still **recognises** that she has a **duty** to her **father** and to her **husband** (1.3.180-187) which would be **expected** of a **woman** at that time.

Emilia's claim that adultery could be justified was controversial.

Practice Questions

Q1 'Throughout *Othello*, Shakespeare supports the traditional Elizabethan stereotypes about race, nationality and gender'. To what extent do you agree with this statement? Back up your answer with examples from the text.

Q2 How important do you think the backdrop of the Cyprus conflict is to the plot of *Othello*? Why do you think Shakespeare decided to add it to Cinthio's story? Refer to the text in your answer.

"Where the senses fail us, reason must step in" — Galileo Galilei

If I were to borrow the plot of Lord of the Rings, muck a few things about, add a battle here or there and change a couple of names I reckon I'd get done for copyright infringement, rather than being praised as a literary genius — Some people get all the luck...

Early Critics

Really early criticism probably went something like this — 'Ooo argh bad um mammoth hunter urg'.
This page isn't as early as all that, but it's still pretty early. Basically, 'Othello' initially had very mixed reviews...

Neoclassicists *thought that 'Othello' wasn't a* Proper Tragedy

1) In 1693, **Thomas Rymer** wrote some of the **earliest criticism** of *Othello* in his work *A Short View of Tragedy*.

2) As a neoclassicist, Rymer **compared** Shakespeare's play to **classical literature**, as well as Aristotle's **dramatic theory** in his *Poetics* (see p.46 for more on Aristotle's tragic theory).

3) **Neoclassicists** wanted tragedies to have **tragic decorum** — this meant that:

- **Plot** was **key** — there had to be a **single plot line** and **events** had to occur in a **limited time** and **space**.
- The **characters** (and **women** in particular) had to act **politely** and **contribute** to the **plot's action**.
- The **language** also had to be **appropriate** — **crude words** weren't **acceptable**.
- The **play** and its **characters** had to have a **moral focus**.

Neoclassicists **emphasised** the role of **poetic justice** — the **characters** had to get what they **deserved** because they wanted the plays to have a **moral**. This was an idea that wasn't important in Aristotle's *Poetics*.

Rymer *argued that the play was* Unrealistic

In 'A Short View of Tragedy' Rymer went through 'Othello' scene by scene, picking out every flaw and improbability he sees in the play.

1) Rymer said that *Othello* had **"some humour"** but that the **"tragical part"** was **"a Bloody Farce"**. He argued that the **plot** was **ridiculous** and **improbable**, for example, he thought that the **handkerchief** wouldn't have caused **such jealousy**.

2) He criticised the play's **setting** and argued that the **change in location** from Venice to Cyprus was **unnecessary**. He also questioned the **timing** — Rymer thought there were **time inconsistencies** in the play, and wondered **when** Cassio would have been **able** to sleep with Desdemona.

For Aristotle, unity of time and place was important (see p.46).

3) Rymer also questioned whether Shakespeare's **characters** were **convincing**. He thought that:

- Othello wouldn't have been allowed to be a **general**, or to **marry** a woman of Desdemona's **race** and **class**.
- Iago's **actions** were **unexplainable** — **"never in Tragedy, nor in Comedy, nor in Nature was a Souldier with his Character"**. Rymer thought that Iago was **too eager** for Othello to kill Desdemona, **without any reason** to be.
- Desdemona was too **contradictory** — she's **innocent**, but also appears **worldly** e.g. in **Act 2, Scene 1** (see p.29).
- Cassio's behaviour was **overly-flirtatious** and **courteous**.

4) Rymer **criticised** the **language** for lacking **decorum**, and **objected** to Desdemona's **apparent flirtatiousness** with Iago in Act 2, Scene 1. He accused Shakespeare of **ignoring tragic decorum** just to **appeal** to a **lower-class audience**.

5) He thought there was no **instructive moral** or **poetic justice** because Othello isn't **punished**, so the ending is **"barbarous"**. He saw no **pathos** in Desdemona's **death**, and thought that it just illustrated **"that a Woman never loses her Tongue"** because she **continues** to have **lines** after she is **smothered**.

Samuel Johnson Defended *the play*

1) **Johnson** was an **18th century** critic who was **influenced** by **neoclassicism**. Johnson **agreed** with Rymer that the **change in setting** in *Othello* contradicted **tragic decorum**, but **generally disagreed** with Rymer's views.

2) He **defended** the **characters** as being **realistic**, and argued that:

- The play **demonstrates** Shakespeare's **understanding** of **human nature**. He was **impressed** by **"the fiery openness of Othello"**, **"the cool malignity of Iago"**, and **"the soft simplicity of Desdemona"**.
- Rymer's **main objection** to Iago was that he **contradicted** the **characteristics** of a **stock soldier character**, but Johnson **dismissed** this, and thought that all of the characters **successfully served** their **purpose** — Iago is clearly a **villain** that the audience can **despise**, whilst Othello can be **pitied**.

3) Johnson also **defended** the **plot** and argued that Iago's **manipulation** of Othello was **"artfully natural"** and **convincing**.

4) As a **neoclassicist**, Johnson looked **closely** at the play's moral. He **disagreed** with Rymer that the play had **no moral** and argued that the lesson was **"not to make an unequal match"** and **"not to yield too readily to suspicion"**.

Romanticism

The Romantics weren't a load of loved up individuals — they just belonged to the Romantic period (and some of them were quite depressed). Note the capital R in 'the Romantics' — it makes a lot of difference to the meaning...

Romanticism was Concerned with Emotion and Passion

1) **Romanticism** was an **intellectual movement** in the late 18th century and early 19th century. Romantics focused on **beauty** and the **individual**, and encouraged people to value their **emotions**.

2) The critics in this period were **less concerned** by Shakespeare's **morality** and **tragic decorum** than previous critics. They looked mainly at the **characters** of the play and their **psychological states**.

3) Romantic critics were usually **writers** who wrote about how the individual could be affected by things like **isolation**, **melancholy**, and **personal misery**. This meant that they could **relate** to **Othello** and other **tragic heroes**.

4) Romantic critics greatly **admired** Shakespeare for his **presentation** of **emotion**. **William Hazlitt** said that *Othello* **"excites our sympathy in an extraordinary degree"** and **celebrated** the play for the **"depth of the passion"**.

Romantics Focused on the play's Characters

1) Unlike **previous critics**, the Romantics tried to paint **Othello** in a **sympathetic light**:

- **Samuel Coleridge** argued that Othello didn't **"kill Desdemona in jealousy"** but that it was forced upon him by **"the almost superhuman art of Iago"**. He argued that **any man** would have **acted** in the **same way** with the **same evidence** from someone like Iago who they **absolutely trusted**. He **emphasised** that Othello wasn't **predisposed** to jealousy, but that Iago **introduced** it to him.

- **Hazlitt** argued that Othello is **"noble, confiding, tender"** but becomes passionate quickly and easily. Like Coleridge, Hazlitt **sympathised** with Othello because of his **"generosity"** — Othello initially treats every character with the **same good will**.

© Mary Evans Picture Library

Samuel Taylor Coleridge
(1772 – 1834)

2) The Romantics also tried to **solve the problem** of Iago's **lack of motive**:

- **Hazlitt** described Iago as having **"indifference to moral good or evil"**, but he thought that Iago turns to **evil** because it allows him to **exercise** his **intellect** more **fully**. Hazlitt emphasises the delight that Iago gets **"from the success of his treachery"**.

- Hazlitt also argued that Iago is **motivated** by **"the love of power"**, which Hazlitt believed is **"natural to man"**. He saw Iago as an **extreme example** of something that's **present** in **everyone**.

- **Coleridge** argued that Iago is **"a being next to devil"**, and described Iago's soliloquies as **"the motive-hunting of motiveless malignity"**. Coleridge thought that although Iago **claims** to have **numerous motives** for his **actions**, **ultimately** they are simply **"fictions"** of Iago's **mind** because he isn't **motivated** by **anything**, and is just looking for **excuses** to be **evil**.

  'Malignity' is another word for 'malice' — having an evil disposition.

- **Algernon Swinburne** agreed with Coleridge that Iago's **malice** was **"fathomless and bottomless"**.

Practice Questions

Q1 Aristotle argued that characters should act according to the "law of probability or necessity". In other words, characters' actions should be shaped by "probability" (what most of us would do), or "necessity" (what they're 'forced' to do). Write a critique of *Othello* analysing whether the characters in the play follow this rule.

Q2 Explain what Dr Johnson meant when he said that the moral of *Othello* was "not to make an unequal match". To what extent do you agree with his analysis of the play's message? Give examples from the text in your answer.

Q3 William Hazlitt argued that tragedy "gives us a high and permanent interest, beyond ourselves, in humanity". Assess how successful *Othello* is in achieving this aim. Refer to the text in your answer.

"Why was not this call'd the 'Tragedy of the Handkerchief'?" — Thomas Rymer

Er... because it's not a very good title. Why was not this call'd the 'Comedy of the Four Teens Betwixt Two Points'? Why was not this call'd the 'Tragedy of a Pale Angsty Demon Man with Fangsty'? Why was not this call'd — oh you get the picture...

20th Century Criticism

Nearly back to the present now — and your present is... a lump of coal. You mustn't have been very good this year...
Hang on — this one's for me. Rats. Your present is actually four more pages of criticism. Not great, but it's better than coal.

20th century critics thought that 'Othello' was More Ambiguous

1) **20th century critics** continued to **debate** the play's **characters** and their **actions**.

2) Most arguments **focused** on the play's **protagonist** (Othello) and **antagonist** (Iago). **Critics tend** to **belong** to one of **two main schools of thought**:

> *A protagonist is usually the main character in a dramatic or literary work. An antagonist is a character who provides opposition to the protagonist.*

Othello is a Noble Hero

Critics such as A.C. Bradley maintain that Othello is a **sympathetic** and **noble character** whose **downfall** is caused by a **being** (Iago) who is **pure evil** — his alleged **motives fully explain** his **actions**. They argue that Othello is **not naturally jealous**, but is put under **intense pressure** by Iago.

Othello is Deeply Flawed

Critics such as T.S. Eliot and F.R. Leavis believe that **Othello** is responsible for his **own downfall**, and **downplay Iago's villainy**. These critics argue that Othello **isn't a noble hero**, but is **flawed**, **foolish** and **egotistical**. **Iago** simply **exploits a weakness** that **already existed** in Othello's **character**.

A.C. Bradley was Sympathetic to Othello

> *Bradley defended Othello's jealousy as being entirely plausible for a newly-wed who didn't know his wife very well.*

1) In *Shakespearean Tragedy* (1904) A.C. Bradley wrote that the **tragedy** in the play comes from the fact that Othello is **"exceptionally noble and trustful"** but he's **ruthlessly manipulated** by Iago.

2) Bradley praised Othello's **trusting nature** and pointed out that all of the characters believe that Iago is **honest** so Othello has **no reason** not to trust him. He also praised Othello's **military abilities** and noted that he was **"a great man"** who was both **modest** but also **"conscious of his worth"** — he has no **insecurities** about his **capabilities**, or the **service** he has done for Venice.

3) Bradley wrote that Othello was **"the most romantic"** of all Shakespeare's characters because of his **poetry** and **exotic background**. Bradley said that Othello's **emotions**, whether he feels **love** or **jealousy**, are so **strong** that they **completely take over**.

> *Remember that a 'romantic' is different from a 'Romantic' (see p.57).*

4) Bradley argues that Othello's **weakness** is that his **intense feelings prevent** him from **thinking clearly** about Desdemona's **alleged adultery**. Bradley states that Othello is **"free from introspection"** and although he feels **extreme emotions**, he can't **understand them**.

5) In spite of this, Bradley **denied** that Othello was **quick to jealousy** and argued that **any man** in the **same situation** would have been **"disturbed"** by Iago's **accusations**. He argued that Othello **never falls** from nobility **completely** — the audience still feels **"love and pity"** towards him by the end of the play because of his **nobility**, **capacity** for love and the **"heart-rending"** suffering that's forced upon him.

He argued that Iago was an Artist of Evil

1) Bradley believes that Iago is **motivated** by **pride** and a **need** to **prove** his **"power and superiority"**. He argues that Iago wants to **exercise** his **"supreme intellect"**, and prove that he's an **"artist"** who's incredibly good at what he does. Bradley also sees him as a **very competitive** character.

2) Bradley explains Iago's **behaviour** as an **expression** of **frustration** because he's been **overlooked** in his **life**. This is because he's not a **good person**, even though he's very **able**: **"Goodness therefore annoys him"**.

3) Despite Iago's actions, Bradley points out that he has a **"superficial good-nature"**. Bradley argues that Iago is also **tragic** because his **intellect** and **skilful manipulation backfire** and **ultimately cause** his **own downfall**. Bradley believes that Iago is **defeated** by the **"power of love"**, something that he **couldn't understand** because it was not **within him**.

4) Ultimately though, Bradley sees Iago as **"a thoroughly bad, cold man"** whose **"supremely wicked"** actions **destroy** Othello by turning his **virtues against him**, while **simultaneously** causing his **own downfall**.

20th Century Criticism

T.S. Eliot Disagreed with Bradley

T.S. Eliot
(1888 – 1965)

1) In 1927, **T.S. Eliot** wrote that he had never read a **"more terrible exposure of human weakness"** than Othello's **last speech** in **Act 5, Scene 2**, lines 334-352.

2) Eliot saw an **"attitude of self-dramatization"** in Othello's final speech. He thought that Shakespeare **presents Othello** as **facing** his **downfall** with an **awareness** of how he **appears** to the **audience** and the **other characters**.

3) Eliot saw this speech as evidence that Othello is **anything but noble** and argued that he spends the final scene of the play **"endeavouring to escape reality"**. Eliot believed that Othello was trying to **delude himself**, and in doing so he manages to **fool the audience** and the **other** characters into **thinking** that **he is noble** when **he is not**.

4) Eliot argued that by the time Othello delivers his speech he has **stopped** thinking about Desdemona **"and is thinking about himself"**. Eliot thought that Othello's **attempt** to **remind** the **Venetians** of his **great service** was **inappropriate**, and that he was simply *"cheering himself up"*.

F.R. Leavis was also Unsympathetic to Othello

Leavis's 'Diabolic Intellect and the Noble Hero' openly criticised Bradley's assessment of the play.

1) In 1937, **F.R Leavis** argued that **Iago's role** as a **villain** in the play had been **over-played** by **previous critics** like Bradley. He said that **Othello's downfall** was the result of his **own weaknesses, not Iago's manipulation**.

2) Leavis thought that **Iago's success** isn't due to his **"diabolic intellect"** but because of Othello's **"readiness to respond"** to Iago's accusations. His argument revolves around the **assumption** that Othello **already has a weakness** which makes him **vulnerable to jealousy**.

3) Unlike Bradley, Leavis argued that Othello becomes **violently jealous very quickly**. Once Iago starts to **poison** his mind, Leavis believes that Othello **"yields with extraordinary promptness"** to **jealousy**.

4) This **undermines** the idea that Othello is a **noble hero**, and presents him as **"tragically pathetic"**. Leavis believes that Othello has no **"self-knowledge"** which is both **"humiliating and disastrous"** for him.

5) Despite Othello's **lack** of **introspection**, Leavis saw him as **self-centred**. He **agreed** with Eliot's idea that Othello becomes **preoccupied** with his **own emotions** in **Act 5, Scene 2** and has a **general tendency** to be **egotistical throughout** the play.

Both Leavis and Bradley agreed that Othello lacked self-knowledge.

- In this argument, Iago is **inevitably reduced** to **"a necessary piece of dramatic mechanism"** — his **role** in the play is to **accelerate** the **tragedy** through his **actions**. For this to work, Iago had to be a **convincing character** with the **appearance of "cunning devilry"**.

- Leavis argued that Iago's **power** comes from something that's **already inside** Othello which Iago **brings** out: **"the mind that undoes him is not Iago's but his own"**.

Practice Questions

Q1 By examining the character of Iago, assess whether there is a reasonable case for A.C. Bradley's argument that Iago is also a tragic character. Back up your answer with examples from the text.

Q2 Do you think Shakespeare meant to portray Othello as a sympathetic or unsympathetic character? Use critical arguments and refer to the text in your answer.

Q3 F.R. Leavis wrote that "Othello is too stupid to be regarded as a tragic hero." To what extent do you agree with this statement? Give examples from the text in your answer.

"Othello is the greatest poet of them all" — A.C. Bradley

'Mirror, mirror on the wall, who's the greatest poet of them all? Snow White? Oh, come on, really...? She can sing a fair tune, a nice little ditty, but you can hardly call that poetry. Right, I'm taking this thing back for a refund, I don't think it's working properly.'

20th Century Criticism

Only a couple more critical schools left to deal with — Feminism and Historicism, and then one final section... *sigh*.
Here's a joke for making it this far — Shakespeare walks into a bar... the barman says, 'I've told you before! You're bard!'

Feminism and Historicism are Recent Critical Developments

> *Some feminist critics also consider themselves to be historicists.*

1) Feminists and historicists look at how *Othello* fits in with its **social** and **cultural background**.

2) Feminist critics study the **role of women** in **literature**, and how this **reflects** the role of **women** in the **wider society**. Historicists examine the context of a text more generally, looking at how it fits in with its **social, political, economic** and **religious background**. They argue that **every text** is **influenced** by the **context** it was **produced** in.

3) Historicists and feminists also study the issue of '**otherness**' in the play.

The Idea of Otherness

A lot of **modern critics** talk about '**otherness**' in *Othello* — this refers to **people** or **things** that don't **fit in** with **social norms**. Being an '**other**' means being **outside** this **norm** and **excluded** from **society** as a **result** e.g. **Desdemona** and **Othello clash** with **social norms** because of **Othello's race** and **Desdemona's rebellion**.

Some critics think that 'Othello' Confirms the Traditional Patriarchy

1) **Marilyn French** argues that *Othello* is a **masculine play** — it **rejects female sexuality**, and Othello and Iago are "**masculine**" because they believed in what Elizabethans saw as **male characteristics** e.g. **reason** and **power**.

2) French thought that the play **confirms** that **men held** all the **power** in **society** — Iago holds women "**in contempt**", while Desdemona **accepts** "**that she must be obedient to males**". French pointed out that all of the characters who even **slightly encourage female independence** (for example Emilia) are **destroyed** by Iago.

3) **Lisa Jardine** said that **Elizabethan drama** only provided a **male viewpoint**. She thought that Desdemona was **punished** for being "**too-knowing**" and "**too-independent**". Jardine saw Desdemona's death as a **lesson** in **what happens** if the **male hierarchy** is **disobeyed**.

> *A patriarchy is a social system where the men are in control and have all the power.*

A Historicist View

Leonard Tennenhouse also argued that Desdemona's **death** is an example of **silencing** the **rebellious female voice**. Tennenhouse argued that the **tragedies** in this era often use **violence** against **women** who **challenged** the **patriarchy**. Tennenhouse claims that the women in these plays continue to "**demand**" their **own deaths** or **blame themselves** for their **murder** (just as Desdemona does in **Act 5, Scene 2**).

Other critics think that it Challenges Social Attitudes

1) **Karen Newman** argued that Desdemona's **decision** to marry a black man is portrayed as "**heroic rather than demonic**" and that the play **challenged traditional views** about **interracial marriage** in **Elizabethan England**.

2) Newman thought that *Othello* has a **mixed message**:

- She argued that *Othello* is part of the **traditional patriarchy**, but **challenges** it too. Even though Desdemona **suffers** the "**conventional fate**" of a "**desiring woman**", the play **challenges social attitudes** because Shakespeare presents her **love** for Othello in a "**sympathetic**" **light**.

- Newman thought that Othello **internalised** the "**masculine fear**" of **femininity** in order to be accepted into Venetian society. Othello sees femininity as a "**greedy mouth**" and **fears female sexuality**, saying that Desdemona **devoured** his stories. Othello believes Desdemona has **committed adultery**, because she has already **gone against social convention** in marrying a **black man**.

3) **Stephen Greenblatt**, a **historicist** critic, thought that Desdemona's **marriage** was an attempt to **gain 'power'** in a society where she is **ruled** by **men**. He agreed that Othello finds Desdemona's **sexuality worrying** because it goes against the "**obedience**" expected of women — Othello feels like he **has** to **punish** her.

4) **Ania Loomba** argued that Desdemona becomes an '**other**' when Othello **condemns** her as an **adulteress** — she becomes an **outsider** because she has been **rejected** by both her **husband** and **society** because of her **perceived actions**. Loomba argues that *Othello* should be used to look at the "**sexism**" of Shakespeare's **society** in **relation** to **modern-day issues**, rather than being seen as **confirming** or **challenging** the **patriarchy**.

20th Century Criticism

Many modern critics think that *Sexuality* is *Very Important* in 'Othello'

1) **Valerie Traub** thought that the play shows how **Elizabethan women** were **defined** by "**their sexual activity**" and their **relationships** to **men** — they were seen as **virgins**, **wives**, **widows** or **whores** (see p.38 for more on gender).

2) Traub argued that Shakespeare was **concerned** by "**unregulated female sexuality**", a **common male insecurity** in **Elizabethan England**. She argued that Iago is **successful** in **manipulating Othello** because he **takes advantage** of real male **social concerns** of the time about **women**.

3) Greenblatt argued that Desdemona's **sexuality** troubles Othello, and makes him **question everything** he **knows**, including **himself**. This **effectively** undermines Othello's "**carefully fashioned identity**" and leads to his **downfall**. He also suggests that the **passion** between Othello and Desdemona is based on **lust**.

4) **Newman** seems to agree with this idea, arguing that Desdemona is **attracted** to **Othello** because of his **sexual 'otherness'** — she finds him **attractive** because he is **different**.

Greenblatt acknowledges that Iago also plays a key role in undermining Othello's identity.

Critics think the play *Questioned Racial Stereotypes*

1) **Newman** thought that Othello's portrayal is both "**heroic and tragic**" when other black characters were generally portrayed as "**villain[s] of low status**" on stage (see p.1-2).

2) **Loomba** argues that Othello's feeling of **belonging**, but also of being an 'other' makes him "**near schizophrenic**" — by the end of the play Othello sees himself as **both** a **defender** and an **enemy** of the state. She thought that Othello transforms from being **accepted** by a **white Venetian society** to being a "**total outsider**" — his **marriage isolates him** because it goes **against social norms**.

3) **Alan Sinfield** agreed that *Othello* **highlights** how **Elizabethan society** viewed **black people** as the '**other**'. Sinfield argued that Othello **recognises himself** as the "**base Indian**" (5.2.343) at the end of the play and **kills himself** because he has been **conditioned** to **defend society against** the 'other' which he has become.

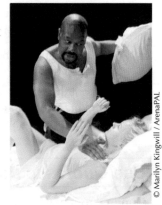

© Marilyn Kingwill / ArenaPAL

4) **Louis Montrose** also thought that *Othello* shows how **Elizabethans** rejected **different races**. He argued that "**exclusion**" from society either made the 'other' **embrace** "**the dominant culture**" in an attempt to be **accepted**, or **actively oppose** it. This is **why** Othello initially **embraces Venetian culture**, but then **rejects** it.

Critics have also looked at the *Presentation* of *Religion*

1) **Desdemona** is a **Christian** and Shakespeare also **emphasises Othello's conversion** to **Christianity** when he talks about "**Christian shame**" (2.3.166). Critics have compared **Desdemona** with **Christ** because she's described as "**divine**" (2.1.73) and is associated with **innocence**, especially in her **death**, which is presented as a **sacrifice**.

2) Othello is **guilty** of **several sins** that would **damn him** to **hell** — he **commits suicide** (which is **against God's law**) and **murder**. His **suicide** could show that he **can't escape** his **origins**, and he even begins to **associate himself** with "**a turbanned Turk**" (5.2.349).

3) **Othello** has also been compared with **Judas**, because he **betrays Desdemona**, and, in the **First Folio**, the line "**base Indian**" (5.2.343) was printed '**base Iudean**' (Judean), which connects him with **Judas Iscariot** (who was from Judea).

It could be argued that 'Othello' reaffirms Christian morality, as it presents love and faith positively, and pride and jealousy negatively.

Practice Questions

Q1 Marilyn French argued that "it would be impossible for Iago to seduce Othello if Othello did not already share Iago's value structure." To what extent do you agree with this statement? Back up your answer with examples from the text.

Q2 A lot of feminists and historicists have emphasised the importance of sexuality in *Othello*. Do you agree that Othello and Desdemona's relationship is based solely on sexual desire? Refer to the text in your answer.

"... nothing comes of nothing, even in Shakespeare" — Stephen Greenblatt

In fact, this is a pretty sound way to approach life... nothing ever comes of nothing — so get studying. Learning all of these critical arguments isn't critical (HA) to your success, but learning some of them sure could come in handy in the exam or in an essay.

Writing About 'Othello'

Even though 'Othello' is a complicated play, there's no need for your essays to be incredibly complicated too.
In fact, as with all essays, there's a simple but effective structure that you can follow in order to do well...

Use a *Plan* to *Structure* your *Argument*

1) **Before** you **start planning**, pick out the **key words** in the **question** so that you can **focus** on the most **important points**.

2) Once you've **worked out** exactly what the question's **asking**, you can start to **plan your argument**.

3) The **best essays** follow a **clear structure**:

- Your **introduction** should set out your **argument clearly** and **effectively** — it's the reader's **first impression** of your essay, so make sure it's a **good one**.

- Each **paragraph** should consider **one key point** of your **argument**. Don't try to cram everything into a couple of long paragraphs — you should consider **each point properly**.

- Every **paragraph** needs to **develop your answer** and each one should **follow on clearly** from the one before — this way your argument will be more **persuasive**.

- Your **conclusion** should **summarise** your **argument clearly** and **concisely**. Give a **final answer** to the **question** and **your personal response** to the text.

4) Plan your **argument** by making a **list** of **all** your **points** and the **evidence** that you're going to use to **back up** each one — this means that your argument will be **supported** all the way through.

5) Work out the **best order** to **tackle** your points so that the essay **flows naturally**. Try **linking** your **paragraphs** by placing **similar topics** next to each other — you could use **bullet points**, **tables** or **spider diagrams** to organise your ideas in your plan.

Use *Quotes* to *Back Up* your *Points*

Quoting from both the **play** and **critics** is a good way of **backing up** your **argument**:

If you're quoting from the **play**, **analyse** the quotes, rather than simply **listing** them. Tell the reader what it **shows** and how it **supports your argument**. Avoid using **long quotes** with lots of **ellipses**.

Desdemona can be seen as a weak character who simply obeys the men in the play: "It was his bidding; therefore... / Give me my nightly wearing, and adieu. We must not now displease him."	
Desdemona can be seen as a weak character who simply obeys the men in the play, because she's keen to do Othello's "bidding" and is concerned that she "must not now displease him."	

Be **selective** if you're quoting a **critic** — it shows your reader that you're using a critic's argument to make a **valid point**. It also shows that you **understand** that it's the **argument** that's **important**, and not the fact that you can **remember** lots of **quotes**.

F.R. Leavis argued that Iago is "not much more than a necessary piece of dramatic mechanism" and said that he's simply a "villainous person... a not uncommon kind of grudging, cynical malice".	
F.R. Leavis argued that the character of Iago is no more than a "dramatic mechanism" who exists to bring out Othello's jealousy. Leavis argued that Iago is not purely evil, but is simply a "villainous person".	

You need to make **critical quotes part** of your argument rather than simply using them **as your argument**. Don't be afraid to **challenge** critical views with your **own opinions**. You can **evaluate** the **strengths** and **weaknesses** of **critical approaches** as you **develop** your **answer**. Remember that if you're writing an **undergraduate essay** you'll need to **reference** your critics **properly**.

Writing About 'Othello'

There are **Five Key Things** to **Think About** when **Writing** an **Essay**

CULTURAL AND HISTORICAL CONTEXT	Look at the **influences** that **shaped** the **text** and the **author's opinions** and **writing style.** Consider how the context would have **affected** the **audience** it was written for. Read some **Historicist critics** to **understand** the **importance of context** (see p.60-61).
ANALYSING FORM AND STRUCTURE	Look at the **genre** (e.g. whether it's a **tragedy** or a **comedy**) and its **form** (e.g. a **play** instead of a **poem** or **novel**) and look at how these **affected** the way the text is **written.** When looking at the **structure**, you should **consider** how the **plot unfolds**, how the text is **shaped** by **stanzas, scenes** and **act divisions** as well as the **setting** and **passing of time** (see p.47).
CLOSE ANALYSIS OF LANGUAGE	Look at **short extracts** or **scenes** to **analyse** the **language** that the author uses to **create** a **certain effect.** This could involve looking at things like **wordplay, rhythm** and **alliteration.**
A RANGE OF CRITICAL OPINIONS	Consider **different critical approaches** to the text, **analyse** their **arguments** and decide if you **agree** or **disagree** with them. **Critical opinion** is a useful way to **support** your arguments.
THE RELATIONSHIP BETWEEN DIFFERENT TEXTS	Look at **other works** that share the **same form** or **themes** and see how **other authors** approach them. It's also **helpful** to look at **other works** by the **same author.**

A-Level Examiners are looking for **Different Skills**

To get **top marks** at **A-level** you need to make sure that you **understand** what the **examiners** are looking for in **your work.**

An informed and creative answer

You need to write **clearly, accurately** and with **good spelling.** Your work must show **creative thought, answer the question,** and be **backed up** with a good **knowledge** of the **text.** You should use **technical terms** where it's **appropriate** (e.g. iambic pentameter, blank verse, soliloquy).

Analysis of how meaning is created

You need to **analyse** in **detail** the **different** ways in which a writer shapes meanings in a text. Things to think about include **structure, form** and **language.**

This all applies to A-Level English Literature only — if you're studying Othello for English Language and Literature, then you'll be assessed on different skills.

An understanding of the text's context

You need to **understand** how **context** might have **influenced** the text. **Explain** the **impact** of the **historical, cultural** and **literary** context on the **author** and the **audience.**

Comparisons with other literary texts

You need to **compare** and **contrast different texts** with one another.

An explanation of different interpretations

You should give a **reasonable personal response** to the texts as well as taking into account **other interpretations.**

"The roots of education are bitter, but the fruit is sweet" — Aristotle

My teacher told me this at school and cleverly I replied, 'What if the fruit is a lemon?' The teacher wasn't happy. The saying might work if you made the lemons into lemonade — 'The roots of education are bitter, but the fruity, carbonated sugary drink is sweet...'

Writing About 'Othello'

On the next two pages are some hints and tips for how to write an essay on 'Othello'.

Pick out the Key Words in the Question

You could talk about the tradition of 'Vice' characters in Morality plays.

You could talk about critics such as Coleridge who have seen Iago as a "motiveless malignity".

You can use a range of textual evidence to argue whether or not Iago has plausible motives.

'Iago exists purely as a dramatic device; he is not a plausible character with believable motivations.' To what extent do you agree with this view?

Your answer needs to come to a conclusion that clearly evaluates the statement.

You could show how Shakespeare's language makes Iago's motivations seem more like excuses.

Introduce your Argument in the Introduction

You might **start** like this:

> Iago is an incredibly complex character. He is manipulative and a habitual liar which makes it difficult for the audience to get an accurate picture of his motivations. Shakespeare may have intended Iago to mislead the audience in the same way that he deceives the characters of the play. As a result, there is evidence that Iago is a character whose ambiguities make him plausible, but also that he is simply a dramatic device.

Referring to the terms used in the question shows your answer is focused.

This introduction is **good** because it **sets the scene** for the rest of the essay — the **reader** knows that the essay will discuss **Iago's motives** and the fact that the character's **complexities** mean that he's **open** to **interpretation**.

Make your First Paragraph about the most Important Point

The **first paragraph** should **expand on** the **point** made in the **introduction** more **fully**:

These short quotes show good textual knowledge and help support the argument.

> Iago claims to have numerous motives in the play, for example, in the first scene he says that he is angry that Othello has made Cassio his lieutenant, insisting "I am worth no worse a place". Later in the play, when Iago is alone on stage, and has no reason to lie, he also claims that he believes Othello has "twixt my sheets / ...done my office". Both of these examples suggest that Iago's motivation is jealousy, and Iago could be seen to confirm this in Act 3, Scene 3 when he tells Othello "oft my jealousy / shapes faults that are not there". Even though he's encouraging Othello's own jealousy, it could still be seen as an admission that Iago is jealous.

This paragraph starts to provide **textual evidence** for Iago having a **believable motivation** in the play and so it **makes sense** to go on to consider the other side of the argument and provide **similar evidence** for a **lack of motivations**:

> However, although Iago suggests motives for his attacks on Othello, they don't seem to justify the hatred he feels towards his general. When Iago is made lieutenant in Act 3, Scene 3, he continues to persecute Othello even though his anger at being passed over for promotion is no longer a motivation. Iago also admits that he knows "not if't be true" whether his wife's had an affair with Othello, which makes the audience question whether any of Iago's stated motives are genuine. His declaration of silence at the end of the play, "From this time forth I never will speak word", suggests his actions cannot be explained, providing evidence that he is just a dramatic device.

This paragraph **questions** whether Iago's motives are **legitimate**, with lots of **textual** evidence.

Writing About 'Othello'

Consider other Relevant Works

It's useful to think about **recurring themes** in other **Shakespeare plays** that can **back up** your **argument**.

> Considering how Shakespeare might have been influenced shows knowledge of the play's context.

> This shows a good knowledge of other relevant works.

It's likely that the character of Iago was influenced by the 'Vice' character in morality plays that were still popular in Shakespeare's time. This character was a dramatic device who the audience could easily recognise as a personification of evil. Shakespeare was familiar with this literary tradition, and used it in some of his other works such as 'Richard III'. In this play, Richard III directly compares himself to a 'Vice' character. Shakespeare may have intended the audience to interpret Iago in the same way, rather than as a plausible character whose motivations had to be believable.

It's **important** that any **references** to other plays **add** to your **answer**. Some questions will ask you to **compare** *Othello* to **other works** (see p.66-67), so you'd need to **refer** to your comparison text **throughout** your essay.

Back Up your Points with Critical and Textual Knowledge

Use **critics** to **support** your argument, but don't be afraid to **challenge** their opinions if you **disagree**:

> Using individual critics is good — you don't have to quote them directly but make sure you get their arguments right.

Many critics have supported the idea that Iago represents 'Vice', or the Devil, and Iago's motives have often been questioned. Samuel Taylor Coleridge argued that Iago is a "motiveless malignity", because he commits evil acts without sufficient reason. Critics that believe that Iago is more than a dramatic mechanism tend to argue that his motives are less obvious than those stated by the character. Many critics, for example, argue that Iago is motivated by a desire for power.

> It would have been better to use a specific critic and go into more detail.

This is **good**, but rather than just **stating** a critic's opinion, you need to **develop** it and **analyse** it **yourself**:

F.R. Leavis believes that Iago is a "necessary piece of dramatic mechanism". Leavis's argument is shaped by his belief that Othello is the cause of his own downfall. Leavis thinks that Othello's inherent flaws and insecurities lead him to jealousy, so Iago exists as a catalyst to bring out his suspicions. However, Leavis's argument could be seen to underplay Iago's role, as the text itself suggests that Othello is "one not easily jealous". This undermines the argument that Iago is simply a dramatic device.

> This explains what you think is problematic about their interpretation.

This is much better because it **engages** with the critic and **applies** his view to the **text**.

Your Conclusion should Concisely Summarise your Argument

The conclusion doesn't need to introduce any **new ideas** but should put forward a **balanced answer** to the question:

> This is good because it directly answers the question.

Iago could be considered a plausible character with believable motives, although his stated motives seem to be insufficient justification for his cruelty. In Act 1, Scene 1, Iago claims that he does not act "for love and duty, / But seeming so, for my peculiar end", suggesting that he has private motivations which he refuses to share. Alternative motives could be a hunger for power, or his racist views, though Iago's deceptive nature makes it difficult to provide firm evidence. Alternatively, Iago could be a dramatic device because Othello succumbs to jealousy so quickly which could suggest that he simply brings out jealousy that was present in Othello from the start. Ultimately there is no reason why Iago cannot be both a believable character with plausible, but hidden, motives, as well as a dramatic device to bring out Othello's jealousy.

This conclusion is **concise** and provides a **reasonable argument** that **answers** the **question**.

Comparing 'Othello'

'Othello' addresses so many of the major themes in literature that it can easily be compared with different texts.
You'll need to consider things like genre, theme and language. If you're stuck for ideas, then this is the page for you...

How to **Compare Different** 'Othello' **Productions**

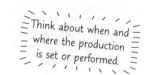
Think about when and where the production is set or performed.

1) If you're comparing **different productions** of *Othello*, it's a good idea to study some **performance criticism** to get an **idea** of the types of thing you can look at.

2) Every director of *Othello* has a **different interpretation** of the play, so there will always be something to **compare** and **contrast**. You might consider:

- **What the production has cut out** — *Othello* is a **long play** and is sometimes **abridged**. Looking at what a director cuts out **reveals** which **parts** they think are **more important**.
- **What the production has added in** — some productions **add scenes** or **dialogue** to make **more sense** of the **ambiguous elements** in the play. This shows what the **director** wants to **emphasise**.
- **How it presents the ambiguous issues** — some directors try to answer the **unanswered questions** by presenting scenes in a **certain way** e.g. **Oliver Parker's** film seems to exaggerate the **homoeroticism** between Iago and Othello to suggest that Iago's **actions** are **motivated** by **love** for Othello (see p.45).

3) It's useful to compare and contrast **different types** of production:

- **STAGE PRODUCTIONS** — look at how **costumes** and **casting** are used to **change** the play's **focus**, e.g. in 1997 **Patrick Stewart** starred as a **white Othello** in an otherwise **black cast** to **challenge racial stereotypes**.
- **FILM PRODUCTIONS** — look at how films make the most of the fact that they aren't **limited** by the **stage**, e.g. **Parker's** film repeatedly shows Iago next to **open fires** to suggest that he's **connected** to **Hell** and **Satan**.
- **ADAPTATIONS** — *Othello* has been **remade** in **different ways**, e.g. Geoffrey Sax's 2001 TV adaptation set the story in a **modern-day police force** (see p.45). Looking at how the play is **re-imagined raises new issues**.

How to **Compare** 'Othello' with other **Shakespeare Plays**

1) The easiest way to compare *Othello* with other **Shakespeare plays** is by looking at how Shakespeare **addresses** different **themes**. This shows how his **opinions** have **changed** over **time**.

2) Here are some **possible comparisons** you could make based on **themes** in *Othello*:

- **Race** (e.g. *The Merchant of Venice, Titus Andronicus*) — Look at how **ethnic minorities** are portrayed differently.
- **Jealousy** (e.g. *Macbeth, The Winter's Tale*) — Consider how **jealousy** is presented as a **destructive force**.
- **Dangers of Language** (e.g. *Richard III, Hamlet*) — Analyse how **language** is used to **manipulate** people.
- **Gender roles** (e.g. *Twelfth Night, The Taming of the Shrew*) — Look at how **gender stereotypes** are **addressed**.
- **Madness** (e.g. *King Lear, Hamlet*) — Contrast Shakespeare's **presentation** of **feigned** and **real madness**.
- **Murder and suicide** (e.g. *Julius Caesar, Romeo and Juliet*) — Consider the **morality** of **murder** and **suicide**.

3) Shakespeare's plays **share** many **common themes**, but this should give you an **idea** of the **links** you could make — there are plenty more **comparisons** and **plays** you could look at.

How to **Compare** 'Othello' with other **Tragedies**

Think about comparing Shakespeare with other playwrights from the same era such as Christopher Marlowe. His play 'The Jew of Malta' deals with issues of race.

1) *Othello* is **sometimes compared** with plays like *Equus* by Peter Shaffer where the **protagonist** feels like an **outsider**, or with plays where the **hero's downfall** is brought about by a **manipulative villain**. Some of the **things** you could look at are:

- **Tragic Flaws**
- **Catharsis**
- **The Protagonist**
- **The Antagonist**
- **Feelings of Isolation**
- **Love and Relationships**

2) **Aristotle's** *Poetics* is a **useful guide** for **comparing tragedies**. Aristotle **outlined** the **structure** and **qualities** of tragic drama — the **criteria** that **neoclassicists** used to **analyse** *Othello* (see p.46).

Comparing 'Othello'

Comparing 'Othello' with Plays of Other Genres

COMEDIES
- The way in which **similar themes**, such as **love** or **gender**, are **presented** in comedies would provide an **interesting comparison**. You could look at the **contrasts** in **language** and **tone** in each **play**.
- Arguably, a **miniature comedy** is played out in *Othello* until **Act 2, Scene 1** — there's a **newly married couple**, a **stereotypical foolish old man** (Brabantio) and lots of **sexual innuendo**. This would provide a good **starting point** if you wanted to compare the play with a **comedy**.

HISTORIES
- **History plays** draw their **inspiration** from **historical events**, especially times of **historical change**.
- Although they are **rooted** in **factual history**, history plays share a lot of the same **stylistic** and **artistic devices** with other plays. You could **consider** whether the **playwright** has tried to make their history play **fit** into the more **established tragic** and **comedic** genres e.g. *Richard III* uses a 'Vice' character similar to Iago.

There are many other **dramatic genres** — **approach comparisons** by looking at how the **writing style** is **different** from *Othello*.

How to Compare 'Othello' with Other Forms of Literature

Poetry

1) If you're comparing *Othello* to a **poem**, you could focus on the **different requirements** of the two **forms** (**play** and **poem**). A lot of *Othello* is written in verse so you can make **form, style** and **language comparisons**.

2) Because poems are generally a lot **shorter** than *Othello,* you could **pick short extracts** from the play that share **similar themes** to the poem, but which provide a **good contrast** in terms of **language** and **style**.

3) Some of **Shakespeare's poems**, such as his *Sonnets,* could provide an interesting **comparison**. Consider how **Shakespeare's writing** varies when he writes in a **different form**. You could explore Shakespeare's **attitude to women** in his **poetry** and **compare** it with his presentation of Desdemona and Emilia.

Prose

CONTEMPORARY WORKS
- Comparing *Othello* with **works** from the **same era** puts the play in its **wider context**, and shows how *Othello* **reflected** the **general mood** of the time. Think about the effect of differences in **form** and **style**.
- A translation of **Cinthio's** *Un Capitano Moro* would provide a **useful comparison** for seeing how Shakespeare **rewrote** the **story** with a **different focus**.
- The character of Iago may have been inspired by **Niccolò Machiavelli's** *The Prince*, which promoted the idea of **pursuing** and **maintaining power** by **any means necessary**. This could show **interesting links** with *Othello*.

MODERN LITERATURE
- Some **themes** in *Othello,* such as **jealousy, love** and **race**, are still **relevant** in modern literature. Because it is a **'domestic tragedy'**, you could make comparisons with **modern novels** which focus on **individuals** rather than issues of kingship, e.g. *To Kill a Mockingbird* by Harper Lee or *White Teeth* by Zadie Smith.
- Look at how **universal themes** like **love** and **jealousy** relate to the **individual** in modern novels — for example, you could study **conflicts** within **relationships**, **feelings** of **isolation** and **attitudes** towards **race**.
- You might also want to consider how the **ideas, attitudes** and **opinions** which are explored in *Othello* have **changed over time** e.g. you could look at how **women** are presented in modern literature.

Practice Questions

Q1 Compare *Othello* to a modern production you have seen or studied, either on stage or on screen. Explore how your chosen production presents the key themes and issues of *Othello* in a modern setting in comparison with the original text.

Q2 Select another Shakespeare play that you have studied and compare and contrast the protagonist in your chosen play with Othello. Look at their key characteristics, their motivations, and consider any differences in how they behave.

"It is better to be feared than loved, if you cannot be both" — Machiavelli

And in short, that's why I leap out at people from darkened spaces... I'm not loved, but I do inspire a mild feeling of discomfort and foreboding, which is about the best I can hope for. Anyway, that's all from me folks, hope you — **BOO!** *I'll get you next time...*

Key Quotes

This page is a gift from me to you... if you've come this far then you deserve it. Use this page for inspiration when you can't quite remember that all-important quote or you need some ideas for a theme-based 'Othello' essay. Enjoy...

Important Quotes

IAGO In following him I follow but myself (1.1.59)

IAGO Thus do I ever make my fool my purse (1.3.377)

CASSIO Reputation, reputation, reputation! O, I have lost my reputation, I have lost the immortal part of myself – and what remains is bestial (2.3.255-257)

OTHELLO Villain, be sure thou prove my love a whore Be sure of it, give me the ocular proof (3.3.356-357)

IAGO He hath a daily beauty in his life That makes me ugly (5.1.19-20)

DESDEMONA A guiltless death I die.
EMILIA O, who hath done / This deed?
DESDEMONA Nobody. I myself (5.2.123-125)

IAGO Demand me nothing. What you know, you know From this time forth I never will speak word. (5.2.300-301)

There are loads of other important quotes — have a look at Section 3 for more quotes relating to themes.

Theme: Jealousy

EMILIA They are not ever jealous for the cause, / But jealous for they're jealous (3.4.156-157)

IAGO Is thought abroad that 'twixt my sheets / He's done my office. I know not if't be true (1.3.381-382)

IAGO O, beware, my lord, of jealousy; / It is the green-eyed monster which doth mock / The meat it feeds on (3.3.164-166)

IAGO I fear Cassio with my night-cap too (2.1.298)

OTHELLO Of one not easily jealous, but, being wrought, / Perplexed in the extreme (5.2.341-342)

Theme: Gender and Sexuality

IAGO Your daughter and the Moor are now making the beast with two backs (1.1.116-118)

BRABANTIO A maiden never bold / Of spirit so still and quiet (1.3.94-95)

BRABANTIO She has deceived her father, and may thee (1.3.290)

IAGO You rise to play, and go to bed to work (2.1.114)

CASSIO And think it no addition, nor my wish, To have him see me womaned (3.4.190-191)

EMILIA They are all but stomachs, and we all but food: They eat us hungerly, and when they are full They belch us (3.4.100-102)

EMILIA I nothing, but to please his fantasy (3.3.296)

OTHELLO I took you for that cunning whore of Venice / That married with Othello (4.2.88-89)

EMILIA I do think it is their husbands' faults / If wives do fall (4.3.85-86)

Key Quotes

Theme: Love and War

OTHELLO	She loved me for the dangers I had passed / And I loved her that she did pity them (1.3.166-167)

OTHELLO	Othello's occupation's gone (3.3.354)	**BRABANTIO**	She was half the wooer (1.3.174)

OTHELLO	I do love thee! And when I love thee not / Chaos is come again (3.3.91-92)

OTHELLO **IAGO**	Now art thou my lieutenant. I am your own for ever (3.3.475-476)	**OTHELLO**	Yet she must die, else she'll betray more men (5.2.6)

OTHELLO	I have done the state some service, and they know't: (5.2.335)	**OTHELLO**	I kissed thee ere I killed thee: no way but this, Killing myself, to die upon a kiss (5.2.354-355)

Theme: Race

IAGO	An old black ram / Is tupping your white ewe! (1.1.89-90)

OTHELLO	Haply for I am black / And have not those soft parts of conversation (3.3.260-261)

DUKE	Your son-in-law is more fair than black (1.3.287)	**BRABANTIO**	Against all rules of nature (1.3.101)

Theme: Honesty and Deception

IAGO	The Moor is of a free and open nature / That thinks men honest that but seem to be so (1.3.393-394)

IAGO	And what's he then that says I play the villain? / When this advice is free I give and honest (2.3.326-327)

OTHELLO	I think my wife be honest, and think she is not, I think that thou art just, and think thou art not (3.3.381-382)	**BIANCA**	I am no strumpet, but of life as honest As you, that thus abuse me. (5.1.122-123)

OTHELLO	My friend thy husband, honest, honest Iago (5.2.153)	**IAGO**	I am not what I am (1.1.66)

Critic Quotes

...the tragical part is, plainly none other, than a Bloody Farce, without salt or savour. **Thomas Rymer**

...we learn from Othello this very useful moral, not to make an unequal match; in the second place, we learn not to yield too readily to suspicion. **Samuel Johnson**

...a great man naturally modest but fully conscious of his worth... **A.C. Bradley**

...I have never read a more terrible exposure of human weakness...than the last great speech of Othello... **T.S. Eliot**

Glossary

alliteration	When a series of words all start with the same letter or sound.
ambiguity	When a word or idea can be interpreted in different ways.
anaphora	The repetition of a word or sequence of words at the beginning of nearby clauses or lines.
antagonist	A character who provides the main opposition to the protagonist, e.g. Iago.
apostrophe	A rhetorical device where the speaker addresses an absent person or inanimate object.
aside	When a character in a play speaks directly to the audience.
blank verse	Unrhymed verse in iambic pentameter.
caesura	A pause in a line, e.g. "So sweet was ne'er so fatal — I must weep."
catharsis	According to Aristotle, the purging of pity and fear that the audience feels at the end of a tragedy.
consonance	When words have the same consonant sounds but different vowel sounds, e.g. "tall / toil".
couplet	A pair of lines in verse that rhyme and have the same rhythm.
cuckold	A man who has an unfaithful wife, but is the last person to find out. This is represented by metaphorical horns which everyone can see but him.
deus ex machina	An unrealistic plot device used to solve problems in a play.
domestic tragedy	A dramatic genre which focuses on the everyday lives of the middle and lower classes.
dramatic irony	When the audience has knowledge of something that the characters on stage don't.
euphemism	When a word is substituted for another which suggests something offensive or distasteful.
feminism	In literature, a movement concerned with how women are presented by writers.
foils	A character who contrasts with the protagonist, a foil emphasises some of the main character's qualities e.g. Emilia's a foil to Desdemona — Emilia's worldliness highlights Desdemona's naivety.
form	The features of a type of literature, such as its rhyme, rhythm or metre.
genre	The type of literature, e.g. drama, tragedy. *Othello* is a tragedy.
historicism	A movement that believes historical context is vital in order to understand a text.
homograph	Words that have the same spelling but a different meaning, e.g. bat (animal / sporting equipment).
homophone	Words that sound the same but have a different meaning, e.g. canon / cannon.
hyperbole	Deliberate exaggeration that's used to create a dramatic effect.
iambic pentameter	Ten syllable lines in which each unstressed syllable is followed by a stressed syllable.
imagery	Figurative language that creates a picture in your mind. It includes metaphors and similes.
introspective	The tendency to inwardly examine your own mental and emotional state.
irony	When words are used in a sarcastic or comic way to imply the opposite of what they normally mean or when there's a big difference between what people expect and what actually happens.
juxtaposition	Placing two things next to each other to create a contrast.
Machiavellian	Being prepared to use immoral behaviour to gain or keep power — as based on the reputation of Niccolò Machiavelli, e.g. Iago is a Machiavellian character.

Glossary

malignity	Another word for 'malice', meaning an evil disposition.
mercenary	Usually a soldier in a foreign army who is paid to provide a service.
metaphor	A way of describing something by saying that it is something else.
metre	The arrangement of stressed and unstressed syllables to create rhythm in a line of poetry.
misogyny	A general hatred of women.
Moor	A word used to describe people from the Barbary coast in North Africa. In Elizabethan times it was usually used to describe anyone with a darker skin tone than a white European.
Morality plays	Allegorical plays where sins and virtues were personified and the protagonist gives in to temptation.
neoclassicism	A movement that compared contemporary drama with classical works.
other	A way of describing people or things that don't fit in with social norms.
oxymoron	A figure of speech that joins two contrasting ideas, e.g. "fair devil".
paradox	A seemingly absurd or self-contradictory statement.
parody	A speech or work that mocks or exaggerates the features of another speaker or literary style.
pathos	A quality in a text which arouses feelings of pity or sorrow in the reader or audience.
patriarchy	A society where men hold all or most of the power, and women have little or none.
personification	A kind of metaphor in which an object is described as if it's a person with thoughts and feelings.
poetic justice	The idea that fictional characters should get what they deserve as a result of their actions.
protagonist	The main character of the work, e.g. Othello.
pun	A play on words that uses ambiguity between words to create humour.
Renaissance	A cultural movement that took place between the 14th and 17th century.
rhetoric	The use of language techniques to make speeches or writing more powerful.
rhetorical question	Where a question is asked when the speaker doesn't need or expect a reply.
rhythm	A pattern of sounds created by the arrangement of stressed and unstressed syllables.
Romanticism	Beginning in the 18th century, a movement which valued beauty, nature and the individual.
sibilance	The repetition of the 'hissing' sounds in words, e.g. 'hush', 'serpent', 'gloss'.
simile	A way of describing something by saying that it's like something else.
soliloquy	When a character reveals their thoughts or feelings when they're alone (or think they're alone) on stage.
superlative	Saying that something is the most, least, best or worst form of something.
symbol	When an object stands for something else, e.g. the handkerchief becomes a symbol of infidelity.
tone	The mood or feelings suggested by the words the writer uses.
tragic decorum	The idea that plays in the tragic genre should follow specific rules, e.g. Aristotle's *Poetics*.
tragic flaw	The character flaw of a tragic hero which leads to his downfall, e.g. Othello's jealous tendencies.
'Vice' character	A character who personifies evil and immorality in morality plays.

Index

Index

Further Reading

It seems like everyone has something to say about 'Othello', even if it's just that it's too long. Critics have been writing about it since Shakespeare's day and directors have been making films of it since... well, since cameras were invented.

Books

Reading what **someone else** has written about *Othello* can help you to work out what **you think** about the play. You can bring **critics** into your **essays** to **support** your argument — you **don't** need to agree with their **opinions** as long as you can say **why not**. Make sure you **reference** your critics properly too if you're writing an **undergraduate essay**.

Thomas Rymer, *A Short View of Tragedy*, 1693 *

Samuel Johnson, *Preface to Shakespeare*, 1765 *

Samuel Coleridge, 'Marginalia on Othello'* and 'Lectures and Notes on Shakspere and Other English Poets', 1810-1818

William Hazlitt, *Characters of Shakespeare's Plays*, 1817

A.C. Bradley, *Shakespearean Tragedy*, Macmillan, 1904 *

Algernon Swinburne, *Four Plays. The Complete Works of Algernon Charles Swinburne*, Heinemann, 1926

T.S. Eliot, 'Shakespeare and the Stoicism of Seneca', *Selected Essays*, Faber and Faber, 1932 *

F.R. Leavis, 'Diabolic Intellect and the Noble Hero', *The Common Pursuit*, Chatto and Windus, 1952 *

G. Wilson Knight, 'The Othello Music', *The Wheel of Fire*, Methuen, 1959 *

John Wain (ed.), *Shakespeare: Othello*, Casebook Series, Palgrave Macmillan, 1971

Marilyn French, *Shakespeare's Division of Experience*, Cape, 1982

Lisa Jardine, *Still Harping on Daughters: Women and Drama in the Age of Shakespeare*, Harvester Press, 1983

Leonard Tennenhouse, *Power on Display: The Politics of Shakespeare's Genres*, Methuen, 1986

Ania Loomba, *Gender, Race, Renaissance Drama*, Manchester University Press, 1989

Karen Newman, '"And Wash the Ethiop White": Femininity and the Monstrous in *Othello*', *Fashioning Femininity and English Renaissance Drama*, University of Chicago Press, 1991

Alan Sinfield, *Faultlines: Cultural Materialism and the Politics of Dissident Reading*, University of California Press, 1992

Valerie Traub, *Desire and Anxiety: Circulations of Sexuality in Shakespearean Drama*, Routledge, 1992

Nicholas Potter, *Shakespeare, Othello: A Reader's Guide to Essential Criticism*, Palgrave Macmillan, 2000

* The asterisked texts can be found in full or extract form in John Wain's *Shakespeare: Othello* — Casebook Series.

Films

Nothing compares to seeing a **stage production** of *Othello* but watching these films will help you get to grips with the **plot** and **language** of the play. It's also interesting to see how different **directors** have **interpreted** the play's **ambiguous** elements and what they've chosen to **emphasise** or **leave out**. Grab your popcorn and take a look at some of these...

Othello (1952): Directed by Orson Welles, who also played Othello, Iago played by Micheál MacLiammóir

Othello (1965): Directed by Stuart Burge, Othello played by Laurence Olivier, Iago played by Frank Finlay

Othello (1995): Directed by Oliver Parker, Othello played by Laurence Fishburne, Iago played by Kenneth Branagh

O (2001): A modern version of *Othello* with Mekhi Phifer and Josh Hartnett, directed by Tim Blake Nelson

Othello (2001): A modern version of *Othello* for television with Eamonn Walker and Christopher Eccleston, directed by Geoffrey Sax

Who's Who in the 'Othello' Cartoon

You should be an expert on 'Othello' by now. But if you want a bit of light relief and a quick recap of the play's plot, sit yourself down and read through 'Othello — The Cartoon'...

Othello

Iago

Desdemona

 Cassio

Emilia

Roderigo

Bianca

Brabantio

The Duke

William Shakespeare's 'Othello'

IN VENICE, OTHELLO, A RESPECTED BLACK GENERAL, HAS SECRETLY MARRIED DESDEMONA, A YOUNG AND BEAUTIFUL VENETIAN WOMAN.

I love Desdemona so much. I can't believe she's run off with Othello — my facial hair is so much better than his.

I hate Othello too! Hmm, I feel a plan coming on...

Roderigo

Iago

IAGO AND RODERIGO VISIT DESDEMONA'S FATHER

Oi, Brabantio!

Bog off, it's the middle of the night.

Othello's bonking your daughter!

Noooooo!

Brabantio

AT THE DUKE'S COURT

Heads-up Dukey, Cyprus is about to be attacked by a load of Turkish ships.

Uh-oh, we'd better send Othello out there. He'll sort it out.

Senator

Duke of Venice

Help! My daughter's been stolen!

Don't worry, we'll catch the scumbag who took her.

It was Othello.

Rats. I like him.

What have you two got to say for yourselves?

We're in love!

That's cute. But I'm still sending Othello to Cyprus.

I'd better go now. Des, you follow on with Iago.

Othello

Desdemona

CASSIO JOINS DESDEMONA AND IAGO IN CYPRUS

I'll make Othello think Cassio and Desdemona are getting it on. That'll make him spit nails.

Cassio

AFTER A BAD STORM AT SEA, OTHELLO MAKES IT TO CYPRUS

Let's party — the Turkish ships were destroyed, hurrah! And I'm so in love with my sexy wife. Rrrrr.

Ha! Not for long, sucker.

Ooh, a party. Don't let me drink, Iago — I can't handle booze.

LATER THAT NIGHT

I'm a tit bipsy.

Here, have another drink son.

Hic.

If I get him really drunk he'll start a fight, then Othello won't like him so much...

Stop running around with your sword out. You're drunk.

Wha'? Lyin' rascal! Take tha'!

Ow!

What on earth's going on? Cassio, I gotta tell ya, you're fired.

Montano

THE NEXT MORNING

So will you put in a good word for me with Othello?

No problem.

Thanks. Here he comes — I'd best skedaddle.

Cassio's a sweetie. You'll forgive him, won't you?

Umm, yeah OK... but I'm a bit busy so it'll have to wait.

Hmph.

It's lucky you don't get jealous like I do.

What do you mean?

Oh nothing, I trust Cassio almost completely. And OK, so Desdemona lied to her dad about marrying you, but that doesn't mean she's lying to you...

Oh my God! They're having an affair!

Bingo!

Oof, my head's banging.

I'll tie this lovely hanky you gave me round your head. Oops, dropped it.

Iago's always on at me to nick that hanky — now's my chance.

Emilia

EMILIA GIVES THE HANDKERCHIEF TO IAGO

I'll plant this hanky in Cassio's room. Mwaha... oh, hello Othello.

This jealousy is making me madder than a ferret in a teapot. I need proof that Dessy's cheating on me.

Well... I saw Cassio using that hanky you gave Desdemona.

Nooo!

OTHELLO QUESTIONS DESDEMONA, THEN STORMS OUT

Othello's acting weird — I think he's jealous.

But I haven't done anything wrong.

So what? Men turn into monsters if they think their wife's cheating. Fact.

ETOT73